A LIFETIME ADVENTURE

A MEMOIR

JACK FRITZ

bookhouse
PUBLISHING

Book House Publishing
2950 Newmarket St., Suite 101-358
Bellingham, WA 98226
Ph: 206.226.3588
www.bookhouserules.com

Copyright © 2020 by Jack Fritz

All rights reserved. No part of this book may be reproduced or transmitted in any form or by any means without written permission from the author.

This memoir is based on the author's recollections, and the personalities and events described are included only to show how important they were in his life's journey.

10 9 8 7 6 5 4 3 2 1

Printed in the United States of America

Library of Congress Control Number: 2020918322

ISBN: 978-1-952483-15-8 (Hardcover)
ISBN: 978-1-952483-16-5 (Paperback)
ISBN: 978-1-952483-17-2 (eBook)

Editor: Larry Coffman
Cover design: Scott Book
Interior design: Melissa Vail Coffman & Scott Book

I dedicate this book to my wife, Jill, who always has stood by me through our ups and downs. She has given me two fine children and worked hard in many jobs that helped to support our family. As a business partner, she does all of the bookkeeping and assists in the management of our apartment building. She has given me so much more than I ever expected, and I thank her for that. I love her and hope that, together, we can continue our adventure for many years into the future.

Contents

Foreword vii
Preface ix
Introduction xi
   Chapter 1: My Heritage 1
   Chapter 2: My Home Town 11
   Chapter 3: Early Beginnings 13
   Chapter 4: Athletics 33
   Chapter 5: Work Ethic 39
   Chapter 6: Education 43
   Chapter 7: The United States Navy 63
   Chapter 8: Building Airplanes 97
   Chapter 9: Social Activities/Dating 107
   Chapter 10: Jack and Jill Went Up the Hill. 113
   Chapter 11: Family Life 119
   Chapter 12: Priest Point Living 123
   Chapter 13: Life in Olympia 133
   Chapter 14: Return to Priest Point 137
   Chapter 15: Penthouse Living 141
   Chapter 16: Building Heavy Machinery 145
   Chapter 17: Washington Natural Gas Company 147
   Chapter 18: Washington State Parks and Recreation 149

Chapter 19: Building the Alaska Pipeline. 153
Chapter 20: Building a Nuclear-Power Plant. 165
Chapter 21: High Technology and Aerospace 167
Chapter 22: Building Computer Tutorials 169
Chapter 23: Aramco—Saudi Arabia. 173
Chapter 24: Plumbing Business 183
Chapter 25: Interim Jobs (Contract work) 185
Chapter 26: Apartment Ownership 187
Chapter 27: Combination-Spares Bowling (My Invention). 193
Chapter 28: Travels and Trips 197
Chapter 29: Living In Arizona 219
Chapter 30: Health 227
Chapter 31: Family Connections 233
Chapter 32: The Future 245
Epilogue 247
Acknowledgments. 249

Foreword

As is usually the case when I get a manuscript to edit, I have no prior knowledge of the author. That was true in the case of the Jack Fritz memoir, too.

But it didn't take long to feel like Jack might be the proverbial "brother from another mother"—given all the commonalities in our lives.

For starters, we're both octogenarians. Then follows a long list of remarkable similarities. We both:

- Are six feet tall, or at least we *were*—before old age took its toll!
- Played football in high school, wearing leather helmets, sans face masks.
- Had injuries end our football-playing days—Jack, a concussion, me, a knee.
- Graduated from Mid-American Conference schools—Jack, Western Michigan, me, Bowling Green.
- Got married in 1963.
- Spent significant time in Baltimore, MD.
- Spent the majority of our lives in the Seattle, WA, area.
- Owned Plymouth Barracuda and Plymouth Fury automobiles.
- Had hernia operations.
- Had basal-cell carcinomas removed.
- Are Hall of Fame nominees at our respective high schools.
- Have been married nearly 60 years to the same woman.

Some dissimilarities are that:
- Jack was U.S. Navy and I was U.S. Army.
- He took swimming to a whole other level, compared with my infrequent splashes in the water.
- I have no desire to go mountain biking, like Jack does, among the rocks, cacti, and diamondbacks in Arizona.
- He and Jill are "snowbirds," who cherish spending Winters at their home in Arizona, while I prefer sticking to the comfort in my "man cave" year-round in Seattle.

A big takeaway from reading about Jack's life is the amazing number and variety of jobs that he had during his working years. When you combine that with the many travel adventures that he had in the Navy—and with Jill—you have ample evidence of a life lived to the fullest!

A side benefit of being a book editor is getting to live vicariously—through the author's writing. You're about to share the same benefit in the following pages.

Enjoy!

Larry Coffman, editor

Preface

I WAS BORN AT THE PEAK of the Great Depression to poor parents, and I had the opportunity, only in America, through hard work and dedication, to survive the ups and downs to propel myself to upper-middle-class status. "Work is the pathway that leads to success" always has been my motto. At age 13, I worked 20 hours a week, six days a week at a restaurant and grocery store. Later on, I worked for my father's plumbing business. During college, I worked 35 hours a week at *The Kalamazoo Gazette*. I've always believed that it's not the winning or losing that counts, it's trying the best you can to meet the challenges in life.

Introduction

Before you read *A Lifetime Adventure*, I want to explain why I didn't structure the chapters in chronological order. It's to distinguish the various experiences of love, work, and play. There were numerous people I admired who helped me learn and meet the challenges along the way. The one word I want to talk about is "discipline." Whatever you want to achieve, it takes discipline to get there. You have to tell your brain that you're not too tired to go to swim practice, or you're not too tired to work and go to college at the same time, or that you can come to work ahead of time and stay overtime—even when you're not paid for that work. Many of these things I had to learn the hard way. I'm not telling my story to preach, only to convey how it affected me.

My paternal grandparents, Mary and William Fritz, on their wedding day.

Chapter 1

My Heritage

My grandmother (on my father's side) was Mary Semrau Fritz, born in 1878 in Friedland, Prussia. She immigrated from Prussia in 1881 with her parents, Othelia Panknin Semrau and August Semrau and seven other siblings. They left Bremen, Germany and traveled third class, sailing on the S.S. Leipzig to the United States. They were examined in Baltimore, MD, then traveled to North Judson, IN, to work on John Radtke's farm, where they adapted to the American way of life. In 1898, Mary met and married my grandfather, William Adolph Kappes Fritz, who was born in 1876 in Chicago. My great grandmother, Pauline Fritz, born in 1847 in Prussia, immigrated in 1865. In 1871 in Pulaski, IN, she met and married my great grandfather Gerhardt Kappes, born in 1827, and also from Prussia.

It's interesting to note that I might have had the last name of Kappes instead of Fritz. However, Pauline Fritz divorced Gerhardt in 1886, after she traveled 40 miles by horse and wagon with her three young children (my grandfather William, being the oldest) to file for divorce. She won, after claiming she was beaten and lacked money to raise her children. Afterward, she took back her maiden name and had her children's names changed to Fritz. William and his wife, Mary Martha Semrau, lived in Chicago, where their first-born son, George, was born. My grandfather became a boilermaker/plumber and worked aboard ships traveling to South Haven, MI. He liked the small lake town and moved his family there in 1902. My father, Harry August Fritz, was the fifth of six boys in the Fritz family. In 1933, I was born in the same house and bedroom that my father was born in on Kalamazoo Street in South Haven in 1910.

South Haven—home of my grandparents—where my father and I were born.

My grandmother (on my mother's side) was Edith Harman Rogers, born in 1886 in Chicago. Her mother was Sophia Berg, born in Sondre Land, Oppland, Norway, and her father was Ole Aalbue from Oppdahl, Norway. My great grandparents were Axel Harman, born in Asby, Ydre, Sweden, and Laurena Berg, born in Sondre Land, Oppland, Norway. Sophia and Axel met in Chicago, after both immigrated to the United States in 1861 and 1862, respectively. My grandfather (again, on my mother's side) was Claude Warren Rogers, born in 1881 in Chatham, IL. My mother, Venita Myra Rogers Fritz, was born in1915 in Chicago, across from Wrigley Field. She married my father in 1932 in South Haven, MI. The Rogers family tree dates back to 935 and lists hundreds of strings of different family names on Ancestry's FamilySearch. One of the women was named Adelaide of Burgundy in 939 which, I'm sure, is where my parents got the name for my sister, Adelaide.

My grandparents, Mary and William Fritz.

In all, my family tree identifies five generations of grandparents. Military service runs deep among my ancestors and is a source of great pride for me. Furthest out in that lineage is George Rogers, born in 1764. He married Elizabeth Randall. George served in the cavalry in the Revolutionary War. His son, James Rogers, was born in 1795 in Guyandott, WV. James was a soldier in the War of 1812 and had two sons. James (named after his father), died in the Battle of Buena Vista in the Mexican War. His brother, John Morgan Rogers, a confederate, was killed in the Civil War in the Battle of Atlanta in Dallas, GA. John Roger's son, Joseph, born in 1855 in Kentucky, was my great grandfather. When the confederate states started the Civil War, Kentucky was divided between south and north. After President Lincoln persuaded the Kentucky legislature to join the Union, John Morgan Rogers traveled to Tennessee and joined the Orphan Brigade and fought in 10 major battles. He also was their brigade violinist. After his death, his parents were given a bounty of land for his sacrifices in the war.

Bell flag from The Revolutionary War.

THE REVOLUTIONARY WAR (1775-1783)

GEORGE ROGERS fought in the revolutionary battle at Yorktown. He was in the cavalry unit of the Virginia Militia. They were called to service and traveled 500 miles to Yorktown, where they defeated the British. It was the decisive victory in the fight for the United States of America's independence. He died in 1858 and his wife, Elizabeth, received a deferred pension for his service in 1859. However, it took many years to receive payment because, at that time, the U.S. government didn't have adequate funds to pay the fighters who defended our country.

My grandmother, Edith Harmon Rogers.

THE WAR OF 1812

JAMES ROGERS (1795-1869) fought in the War of 1812. Great Britain had promised Indian Chief Tecumseh's tribes large parcels of land to help fight the United States of America. Fort Meigs was occupied by the American army. It was at a strategic location in the then-northwestern United States. The British and Indians outnumbered the Americans four to one. After many days of fighting, the fort began to run out of supplies, lead, and powder. At night, a rider slipped through the surrounding enemy and rode off to call for reinforcements. James Rogers was among the 600 cavalry who rode 200 miles to defeat the British and Indians that had laid siege to the fort. Jill and I toured the 1,200-acre reconstructed fort in 2015. It displayed very authentic uniforms and firearms. The site is on the outskirts of Perrysburg, OH, and is the largest reconstructed fort in the United States.

Later in 1814, James Rogers was moved down the Mississippi River to New Orleans to engage in another battle. The Battle of New Orleans was a pivotal point, forcing the British to withdraw their troops and Navy back to Europe so that they could concentrate on the war that was going on there. While in New Orleans several years ago, Jill and I boarded a tour boat and went down river to where the battle was fought. The National Park Service showed us how the troops dug trenches that were fortified with logs and trees to provide an advantage when the British came out from the swamps. The Americans were greatly outnumbered, but the British were exhausted from their long trek through the swamps and were shot down before they could advance toward our forces. This is referenced in the song "The Battle of New Orleans."

During the fighting, a musket ball shattered James Rogers' writing hand and he was put out of action. After being discharged, he began his journey back to his home in West Virginia. Along the way at a local pub, his pouch containing his discharge papers was stolen. When he arrived home, his wife wrote to his commanding officer to substantiate his disability so that he could obtain 60 acres of land as a bounty payment for his disability. My mother obtained copies of these letters from The Library of Congress military records.

THE MEXICAN WAR

JAMES ROGERS, an uncle in my lineage, belonged to the Kentucky Militia. When President Polk called for forces to fight in the Mexican War of 1840-1844, he joined. His enlistment paperwork included his horse, valued at $50, and a saddle, valued at $10. He trekked all the way to Mexico to fight during The Battle of Buena Vista, where he was killed by a Mexican lancer. His father later obtained another bounty of land for his son's sacrifice. We have a copy of the letter from his son's commanding officer stating that it was officially correct. The following poem shows the importance of giving one's life for their country: *"I did my duty. I paid the supreme price. I pray you will remember my sacrifice. My life was short. I did my best. God, grant me peace in my eternal rest."*

THE CIVIL WAR

BEFORE THE CIVIL WAR officially began, there were people who wanted Kentucky to join The Confederacy but the State Legislature followed Lincoln's advice, which urged them remain with the Union. Because of this, many men traveled south to Tennessee to join up with the Confederacy. John Morgan Rogers (1834-1864), was one of these enlistees. They were called The Orphan Brigade. They fought in 10 major battles during the course of the Civil War. There were many lulls between one battle and another, so the troops needed some sort of entertainment. John was the brigade violinist. He was wounded in The Battle of Atlanta, near Dallas. Later that day, he was captured and sent to a Confederate prison camp, where he died. John had married Jane Vaughan, whose father was an Indian, and they had five children.

John Palmer (1821-1866), a farmer, lived near Shiloh, TN, with his wife and four children. When the Battle of Shiloh began, he was not officially in the Confederate army. The first day of the battle, John was working in his fields when he heard the shooting. He wanted to help out in the fight, so he ran to his house, picked up his gun, and sped to the battle. The first day, the Confederates overtook the Union soldiers and forced them to retreat. However, John was wounded and placed in the church that was on the battlefield. The next day, General Grant sent additional troops down the river to Shiloh. They overwhelmed the Confederate lines and, as they approached the church, John limped out, gun in hand, and was mortally wounded. His wife and children subsequently traveled north by wagon back to live with relatives in Illinois. Later, she tried to get compensation for his death but was refused because John was not a registered soldier.

I'm proud of my Indian heritage that goes back five generations to where a Frenchman, whose last name was Cochran (his first name was not available from my mother's records or our search), married an Indian woman. Something happened to incite the Seminole Indian tribe, and they came and killed the father and mother and took my great-great grandmother, Sarah Ann Cochran, born in 1828, and still a baby. The tribe raised her for several years until she was adopted by some neighbors, the Stouts.

And I'm proud of all my relatives who served in the armed forces of the United States of America!

Addie and Joseph Harmon celebrating their 50th wedding anniversary.

The Semrau family.

Great grandmother, Sophia Aalbue, holding grandson, Bud Rogers.

South Haven Main Street in the early 1930s.

South Haven beach, pier, and lighthouse.

Chapter 2

My Home Town

South Haven is situated on the southeastern shore of Lake Michigan. Its aesthetic surroundings and expansive lake makes it a joy to behold. The earliest recorded history tells of the Ottawa, Miami, and Potawatomi Indians tribes that resided in the region. Historians believe the Potawatomi tribe came from the Green Bay area of Wisconsin about 1721. The first white man to settle in what is today South Haven was Judge Jay R. Monroe in 1833. By 1852, the first post office and one-room school house were built. Regular boat service to Chicago was established at this time, too. The railroad came through in 1871, and the number of lumber mills, tanneries, fishing-related activities, and fruit trading increased. South Haven gained recognition as an ideal Summer-vacation spot. The white-sand beaches and easy access to swimming, boating, and fishing, along with the cool breezes that blew in from the lake, drew vacationers from Chicago, Detroit, St. Louis, Kansas City, and cities in Indiana. By 1909, the South Haven Steamship Company and the Pere Marquette and Michigan Central Railways were bringing increasing numbers of visitors from Chicago. Seventeen resorts were listed in the South Haven Board of Trades. Today, the tourist industry is still flourishing. I have the fondest memories of growing up there.

In the baby buggy, being pushed by Beverly Waller.

Chapter 3

Early Beginnings

THE FIRST MEMORY OF MY LIFE was when I was less than a year old. My mother had laid me down for a nap on a bed at Minnie Bouton's boarding house. I rolled off the edge of the bed, hit a flower pot, fell to the floor, and the flower pot hit the back of my head. I still have that scar on my head today.

At Christmas time, I always wanted to help Grandma Fritz decorate the tree, but she never would let me. She always would ask me what we (my parents) had gotten her for Christmas, and she would say, "Just give me a hint. What does it start with?" I'd answer with the first syllable of the first word, like "perc…!" So she knew right away! The other relatives picked up on that, so I always let it be known what they were getting for Christmas, too. Opening presents always was really exciting. My Uncle Harold was a big tease. (All the Fritz's were big teasers!) Once, he gave me a doll that I promptly took outside and threw in the snow. Another time he gave me a pair of rubber pants!

When I was two or three, a little neighbor girl and I were playing, and she stuffed a cherry pit into my nose. The doctor had to remove it. We used to make dolls out of hollyhocks flowers. Another playmate, Beverly Waller, put me into her baby buggy. I had a Pontiac paddle car and rode it around inside the house in the Winter. When I was three or four, my mother was taking me out of the bathtub when lightning struck through our open bathroom window. Luckily, we both were standing on a rubber mat.

When I was about four, we moved to a little rental house on Monroe Boulevard. It was next to a rich family, the Overtons. I played with Sam Overton in the Summers; one day, his nice sailboat drifted out into Lake Michigan. I jumped into our old rowboat and went out and retrieved it for him. Sam and his family really appreciated my rescuing his boat. He also had lots of toys that came in handy during stormy, wintery days.

With my mother.

One Winter, after I was told not to go down to the beach because of the huge icebergs, I did anyway and fell through the ice. One leg was all wet through my heavy underwear, and I came home and got a good spanking. I got lots of spankings over the bathtub with a belt in those days. We moved again when I was about five years old to

602 Maple St. It was a two-bedroom house on the corner of Clinton and Maple Streets, across from the railroad tracks. My father worked in the foundry in town and walked to work every day. We never had a car. My first memories were that the house had a small attached shed with a wooden icebox in it. Once a week, the iceman came and left a one-foot-square block of ice. In the Summer, we kids would grab pieces of ice from the back of the truck to suck on. Later, we got a real refrigerator with a compressor on the top. This was in the Depression, so my father only worked three days a week. On his off days, he hunted and fished a lot to put food on the table.

With my parents at about a year old.

When Dad first took me hunting, I remember the grass being taller than I was. He also would go hunting for snowshoe rabbits with our dogs, Jack and Sport. When cleaning the rabbits in the basement, I held their hind legs while Dad pulled the skin off. I kept sliding from one end of the basement wall to the other end. My mom would can the rabbit meat. Dad took me rabbit hunting once when he borrowed Grandpa Fritz's car. He told me to stay inside and wait for him. I got so cold that I began walking home until someone came along and drove me back to our house. Dad was really worried, but he found me safely at home.

Me at about four years old.

In the Spring, Dad, Uncle Harold, and I went spear fishing for suckers at Deer Lick Creek. I carried the gunny sack to hold the caught fish. Fish kept flying to shore, and I put them into the gunny sack. After the third or fourth hole, I couldn't carry the sack because it was so heavy. We fed the whole neighborhood that day, using Otto Gering's recipe to cook them.

During the Depression, my grandpa, Dad, uncle Harold and other uncles, and I used to drive on the weekends to Saugatuck, 15 miles north of South Haven, to fish for northern pike, catfish, bass, and turtles. But first we went to Deer Lick and other creeks to get chubs for bait. Dad had an eight-foot-long net, with two handles on each end. I remember wading up to my chest and hearing Dad cuss, telling me to move faster up to the shore where we'd fetch them into a five-gallon bucket. I never wore shoes and had to walk through sharp thorny weeds that hurt my feet. The chubs were attached to a three-gang hook and cork and cast out from our rowboat. The fish would chase the bait, bite the hook, and my dad would bring them in. Sometimes a turtle would take the bait, and grandma made turtle soup.

In the boat, ready to go at Saugatuck.

I'd always get bored sitting in the boat for hours at a time. Dad once got mad and said, "Well, swim to shore if you don't want to wait."

I hadn't yet learned how to swim, and the first thing he saw was me in the water, four feet from the boat, beginning to sink. I came up and quickly dog paddled to shore. Dad was almost ready to dive in. Another time, Dad's fishing lure got caught in a bush along the shore. He said to swim in and loosen the lure. I swam in and reached for the lure, and more than 100 bees swarmed at me. I was back in the water fast and didn't receive one sting.

My grandparents, The Fritz's, lived next door on Kalamazoo Street, beside our rented house. They had their garden in the ravine and chickens roamed the backyard. Grandpa cut off the chickens' heads and they ran all around, before finally collapsing. Grandpa had his plumbing shop in the basement of their house. Grandma's sauerkraut was in the basement, too, along with her laundry machine with rollers to rinse the clothes. She would hang the clothes outside on the line to dry. She also took in laundry to help earn some money. I played in the ravine where there was a creek. And I remember playing "shake the dice" and "Old Maid" card games with grandma Fritz.

Thursday was grandma Fritz's bake day. She made delicious loaves of bread, donuts, and apple-coffee cakes. One day, I invited all my playmates into the house when she went to the corner grocery store to buy more flour. We ate most of her donuts, cookies, and coffee cake. She was very mad at me when she returned, as there wasn't much left. She was a very good cook, and I especially liked her sauerkraut and dumplings, goulash, potato pancakes, and schmaltz.

When I was very young, we had two bloodhound dogs named Jack and Sport. I remember many times Dad and uncle Harold used to tease the dogs. My grandparents took in a roomer, Dick Richardson, to help make ends meet during the Depression. He had an upstairs bedroom, and we listened to Gabriel Heater's newscasts and Joe Lewis' prize fights on the radio. Dick was a vet of the Spanish American War.

In 1940, when I was seven years old, the Armistice Day storm unexpectedly swept across Lake Michigan. Three fishing boats (called tug boats) were far out in the lake. The winds and high waves made it impossible for them to return to shore. The Coast Guard boat went to rescue them, but three tugs were sunk and all of the crews drowned. The same morning, my parents had sent me down to the local store for some groceries. It was raining and I had on a large raincoat. A hurricane-force wind suddenly swept under my raincoat, and I was lifted up in the air. Luckily my uncle Harold was driving by and rescued me.

As young kids, we were given rudimentary toys that resembled actual adult building tools. There were peg-pounding boards and wooden wheel-like objects that had holes for straw-like spokes or metal appendages. We also used cards to fabricate miniature rooms, stacking one room atop another until the entire structure collapsed. And whittling wood with a jackknife produced creative forms like spears and arrows—or we just whittled to whittle.

At about age seven, all of us kids decided to build a hut in Terry Mitchell's backyard, using all the wood scraps and cardboard we could find. One day, for reasons no one can recall, we kicked Dave Allers out of our "club" and, of course, out of the hut. So Dave went down to the river, caught a fish, and hid it in the wall of the hut, behind the cardboard. We found out and locked Dave in the hut until he told us where the fish was—and he got rid of it. His scheme must have worked because we let Dave back into the club!

When I was eight and Dick Collins was seven, we were playing on the sidewalk on Maple Street when the Getman kid, who was about 12, bullied Dick. I tried to protect Dick but was thrown down by the bully and injured. My parents took me to the hospital, where the X-ray showed I had a broken collarbone. That was something to have gone to a doctor!

Winter would bring huge snowflakes. I remember how our outside play activities changed, as the landscape turned to snow. I would bring out my American Flyer sled. I grasped it with my hands on either side, ran down the street, leaped down onto the sled, and glided to a stop. We walked several blocks from our neighborhood to a hill near where the Coast Guard master's house was located. We sped down the hill, ducked, and flew under a chain-link fence.

Another Winter activity was ice skating. My first skates were clamp-ons, similar to clamp-on roller skates. They had double blades on each skate. Every winter, the city would flood an area on the south side of town for people to use as a skating rink. Large banks of snow were piled along the sides of the pond. I remember walking six blocks to the area. It was nighttime and the sky was illuminated with a thousand stars. I remember the song, "The stars at night are big and bright, deep in the heart of Texas." I sang it as I began skating across the pond. Sometimes, older kids arranged a "crack the whip" game. Since I was the smallest, they put me at the end of the line. Round and round, faster and faster, they would wind me until I couldn't hold on and was catapulted out onto the snowbanks. They aimed me toward the girls, who screamed as I soared up onto the piles of snow!

When I was nine years old, my parents bought me a pair of hickory skis. We all wore "high tops," a boot that had metal clasps and laces that tied midway up the legs. The bindings clamped onto these boots. In those days, the skis were quite long, which made it difficult to turn. There were sand dunes located six miles south of town. All the trails were straight up and down. Both Winter and Summer, we would ski and roll down, then climb back up, then ski down again.

Another Winter activity was making homemade ice cream. We packed chunks of ice from around the house into the hand-crank ice-cream maker. Everyone took turns cranking the handle until the ice cream was ready to eat. We really enjoyed the taste!

In the Spring, we all went outdoors and played "kick the can," "hide and seek," and "you're it!" Across the street at Bonnie Weaver's house, her mother played the piano and we all played the game "Pop, goes the Weasel" to her music. An odd number of chairs were placed around a table, with an even number of kids. When the music stopped, we all raced for a chair. If you couldn't find an empty chair, you had to leave the game. It was really fun when only one chair remained and two friends had to vie for it—leaving a winner and a loser!

When I was seven, Ms. Wheeler and Mrs. Kellog started a Cub Scout group. The boys all met at the Kellog's house. The club instilled essential character-building habits. When I turned 12, I joined the Boy Scouts of America. I earned several merit badges, the most important one was for Lifesaving, which I completed at Camp Maderin. When I was 15, that training helped me in getting hired as a lifeguard at the South Haven public beaches.

We had lots of hikes and overnight camping trips. A highlight was preparing stew over a burning campfire. One outing was at Allegan Forest, 16 miles from South Haven. Right after finishing our supper, one of the older boys said, "Let's go out and catch some snipe birds." This was my first campout, so I had no idea that I was to be taken advantage of, as I was handed a large open-ended bag. We all left the camp and walked for about 100 yards. They said, "Jack, hold the bag wide open and we'll chase the birds toward you. After you've caught two or three, come back to camp." I stood there and, as I heard them running, I immediately knew that—what's the old saying—I was "left holding the bag!" I wanted to beat them back to camp but ran directly into an old barbed-wire fence. Immediately, three rotten fence posts collapsed, and I was entangled. I quickly got up and ran as fast as I could back to camp. There were four ugly gashes on both of my upper legs. The scoutmasters cleaned them and poured sulphur powder into the wounds and bandaged them. I still have the scars, the largest a quarter of an inch wide. We all decided it was not a good stunt to be playing at night.

My sister, Adelaide, was born on June 25, 1940, when I was eight years old. I was gone all day with an older friend, LeRoy Porter. My parents dropped me at my grandma Fritz's house on their way to the hospital. The town was considered safe in those days, and children roamed for hours. LeRoy and I walked outside of town and eventually came to a strawberry farm. The owner asked if we wanted to earn money picking. I was given a big tray and began to pick. The tray filled quickly because most of the berries were white and not red! The owner was a little upset at our picking the unripe berries. He knew my grandfather and he called him and had him drive five miles out of town to pick us up.

With my new baby sister, Adelaide, born in 1940.

I was nine when World War II erupted. We had just finished supper when the news on the radio began. The announcer stated that the Japanese had attacked Pearl Harbor. Eugene Wheeler and Charles Bronson lived a few houses down the street from us. Eugene enlisted in the Marines and Charles joined the Army. Within a year they both were killed in action. Shortly thereafter, gold stars were displayed in the front windows of their parents' houses. After the war began, household necessities were rationed: Butter was scarce and soon replaced by margarine; stamp books were issued for other scarce foods and gasoline. My friends and I no longer could find Hershey bars at the neighborhood grocery store.

The Indiana Grade School playfield was used to stockpile iron and metal for use by the Army. At recess, we used to jump on the old springs lying in the pile. My father tried to enlist for military duty but was refused because of a blood condition. He also got a deferment because he was a molder at the American Motors Foundry that made engine blocks for jeeps and military trucks. My mother joined the war effort at the Bohn Aluminum plant, where pistons for B-24 bombers were made. Our neighborhood games changed from cowboys and Indian games to simulated military battles. We bought model-airplane kits that consisted of a balsawood framework that was glued together and covered with a thin paper "fuselage."

Aunt Do and her son.

Uncle Harold, who fought in Europe in World War II.

Most everyone bought war bonds to help pay for the military effort. I remember how I paid for my first war bond. At school, the teachers collected our change to buy stamps. Each stamp was placed on a page in a war-bond book, and a totally filled book paid for a bond. I recall buying at least one bond that way. I remember the day that World War II ended and everyone spilled out into the streets. I clambered up onto a two-ton military truck, shouting and waving the American flag. My Uncle Herald came home 10 months after the war ended. He was part of the occupation forces left in Austria.

When I was 10, I visited my Aunt Do in Chicago. I needed more to do than just stay in her house every day and read books, so she gave me 35 cents and told me to take a streetcar to the Field Museum in downtown. I had to change street cars twice to get there. It was fascinating, looking up at the huge dinosaurs and other prehistoric life. When I finished, it was still early in the day, so I walked to the Shed Aquarium, which was along the shore of Lake Michigan. Afterward, I walked along Lake Shore Drive toward the entertainment district of Chicago. Soon I heard exciting music and singing inside of a burlesque theatre. I asked a man standing outside if I could go in to see what was happening. He said "OK, lad, take a look!" It was quite impressive to a 10-year-old kid!

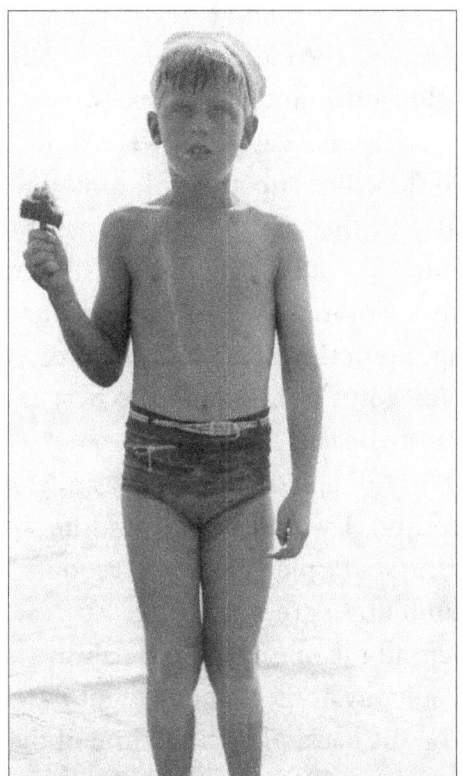
I played on the beach almost every day.

Seems I still had some money left—25 cents—to buy some ice cream and for my return home. But there was some daylight left, so I meandered in and out of cigar stores, clothing stores, and taverns before deciding to catch the trolley back to Aunt Do's house. It was evening when I arrived, and Aunt Do was worried about me. She adored me, especially since she had lost her only son to an illness at my age and her nephew (my mother's brother) to a motorcycle accident. He was 19 and living with her while he was attending the University of Chicago. Whenever she came to South Haven, she would give me a five dollar bill! When I was a young teen, my family and I would drive to Chicago and stay with her for a few days. I'll forever remember that she had a bulldog that constantly let off very offensive smells!

Swimming in Lake Michigan was my fondest Summer activity. Both of my parents worked at defense plants during the war, leaving me time to go to the Lake Michigan beach. The Black River flowed between the south and north piers. The south pier had a wooden diving board, and catwalks were built in the middle of the piers. We would climb up the columns and dive diagonally over the pier and into the lake. My friends and I were constantly throwing rocks into the water, simultaneously diving for them and climbing back out for more rocks. Why someone didn't get hit and drown is amazing! Sometimes, if I had the money, I would buy an apple from "Apple Molly," who made the best caramelized apples and sold them on the beach.

Occasionally, my dog, Boots, would wander out on the north pier. When I'd see him, I would whistle and he would jump off the pier and swim to the south pier, place his feet onto the metal steps of the ladder and climb up to greet me. Afterward, he would follow me home, running behind me on my bike. He always stopped to chase a neighbor's cat on our way home, but one night the cat was waiting for him and jumped on his back. That cured him of that chase!

Boots had his run of the beach all day long, being fed and petted by the Summer vacationers. He never ate his food at home, so we know he was well nourished. Sometimes, when we would get ready to go somewhere in the car, I would tell Boots to get into the car, and he would run out and jump up and through the open car window and sit there waiting for us! If he could have talked, he would have told us some very interesting things, I'm sure, as he was such a smart dog.

Boots.

Boots was a mistake. His mother, Maggie, was a pedigreed English Setter and my father was breeding her to a male English Setter. Since Maggie had been tied up outside, a Collie intervened. There was only one puppy, which we kept and named Boots, because of his white feet. I was eight at the time and, during the Summer, he followed me everywhere. I remember wrestling and rolling in the grass with him as we both grew up.

When I turned 12, my dad bought me a 12-gauge shot gun. The first day of pheasant hunting we placed Boots and Ginger into our 1930 Model-A Ford and drove two miles to hunt. Ginger, an Irish Setter that came to my family after Boots, already was a well-trained hunting dog. Boots, who hadn't had any training, immediately ran, flushing pheasants way out of shooting range. The following day, we left Boots home, and we drove the same two miles to where we had hunted the day before. We had hunted for about an hour when, all of a sudden, Boots somehow appeared. He stopped in front of us, looked up at us with apologetic eyes as if to say. "I'm sorry, I'll do better."

And from that day on, he never strayed out of range again. Boots and Ginger became a good pair. They would run back and forth through the cornfields and flush pheasants out for us. Boots was a terrific dog and a great companion.

On one of my earlier days of hunting, I was separated from my dad and Ginger. Boots and I were hunting, when a pheasant flushed and flew into the air. I shot and the bird fell to the ground. I picked it up and put it into the trunk of the car. After Dad and Ginger rejoined us, I probably said, "Dad, I got my first pheasant." We opened the trunk and right there the bird stood, looking at us! Then Dad rung his neck. That night, after feathering the bird, we found that there were no pellets in it. Dad laughed and said, "Jack, you missed him! He must have been faking a heart attack," Later that week our friend, Don Bobo, wrote an article about my experience in the local paper.

In the Summer, we would ride our bicycles down to the river where the small boats were moored. Dad's flat-bottomed row boat was tied up there. Dick Collins, Dave Allers, myself, and Boots would cast off and row upstream, move under the Highway 31 bridge, and tie up to the shore, next to a big cottonwood tree. A platform had been built for diving into the river. After swimming in the nude, we would continue up river to where the lily pads grew. They had beautiful yellow blossoms. Turtles napped on rocks along the bank, and garter snakes swam by the boat. Finally, the river turned into clogged logs and large rocks. We tied the boat to the shore and explored the woods next to the river. Boots scurried back and forth, smelling the ground and chasing squirrels, so I decided to call this place "Boots Valley." We ate our sandwiches and rowed back to the moorage. These times were very similar to scenes from Mark Twain's books about Tom Sawyer.

Many times we would row out into Lake Michigan and go south for three miles, just out from Deerlick Creek, to the spawning grounds for perch that was called "the rocks." We trailed our fishing lines behind the boat and we caught quite a few of them. I would have to turn the boat around to bring the fish in, and Boots would go crazy! The perch had excellent flavor. We would then row back past the light-house into the Black River. Other times, we fished for perch and other white fish from the pier, using long, bamboo fishing poles and minnows and cray fish for bait. After fishing, we would swim, lay on the hot, sandy beach, and eventually walk back home.

Fall weather brought frost. The multicolored leaves were raked onto the streets and burned. The weather was brisk, and the smell of burning leaves permeated the town. It was time to go see the South Haven High School Rams play football! My parents would give me 25 cents to get into Randcliff Field to see the game. Why should we pay to get into the game when that money could buy popcorn, a soda, or a hot dog? A hole had been dug under the north fence, and we would watch for an opportunity, then scramble underneath, usually when the band was marching down the field. Somehow, we were more interested in playing our own football game behind the grandstand, then heading to the concession stand to buy our treats. When we grew older, like 11 or 12, we would climb the fence and jump down 10 feet to the ground. Luckily we never suffered any broken bones. We did watch the varsity team when the game was close and also at halftime, when the band would perform.

South Haven had one movie theater. My uncle, Ferdinand Semrau, was the ticket taker and usher. He also sold treats at the concession stand. We would wait behind the movie theater until the lights went out, then quickly open the exit door and scamper into the movie. That effort gave us money for treats! I'm sure my uncle knew what was happening.

When I was 11, my parents bought an older, Victorian-style house on the north side of town, which was predominately a resort for Jewish vacationers. Some full-time residents lived in the neighborhood. During that first Summer, I shoveled ashes and other debris from the basement. My parents planned to remodel the house to serve both as a family residence and as a vacation rental during the Summer. My grandfather Rogers came and helped us with the work. A one-bedroom apartment, with kitchen privileges, was partitioned off from the downstairs living and dining rooms. Four additional bedrooms were rented out, too.

Uncle Ferdinand Semrau, left, and my grandfather, William Fritz.

Summer arrived—along with thousands of Jewish vacationers. In order to get the maximum amount of rent from the house, we decided to move into the adjacent garage during the Summer. My father, mother, sister, and I all lived in an area of about 400 square feet. We cooked on a Coleman camp stove and used the upstairs bathroom in the house. The additional income helped to make the mortgage payments. In 1948, my parents sold the house to a Jewish family from Chicago. The new owners agreed that we could stay in the house during the Winter months, rent free, if we did routine maintenance projects, like painting the house.

My father did plumbing work for Mr. Johnson's estate on Doctors Road, five miles south of town. The property sat on a bluff overlooking Lake Michigan and had a creek that ran south of the main estate. A three-bedroom cottage that we lived in during the Summer months was nestled between pine trees and was adjacent to a nearby creek. A screened porch on the lakefront side afforded a 180-degree view of Lake Michigan. A path led down to the beach. Most evenings we ate dinner on the porch, listening to the waves break against the shore. Sunsets with painted clouds presented a relaxing atmosphere. Friends, relatives, and my classmates enjoyed coming to see us.

When I was a lifeguard, I would take my 12-foot aluminum boat from our cottage the five miles to the South Haven beaches. Sometimes a wind would blow up five-foot-high swells. I would position myself fore and aft and cascade up and down the troughs, between the waves. When I reached the cottage, I would carry the boat and motor up the path along the shore. Other times I would ride my bike the five miles to and from work. I painted the inside and outside of the cottage in my spare time.

One day, Mr. Johnson asked me to come over and meet his 15-year-old daughter. She was an attractive, blonde, Nordic girl. We played pool and walked the beach together. Her father was a rich industrialist, and she definitely was from a much higher class of society than me. The next morning, Mr. Johnson and I drove to the South Haven pier and fished for perch. He was a down to earth fellow, and you could never tell that he was a millionaire. I guess that I didn't make that good of an impression on his daughter, because I never was invited again. No problem! Much later in life, I found the delight of my life—another Johnson much prettier and a lifetime partner!

My friend, Jim Morris, lived on the south end of Superior Street. His father made their basement into a very nice bar and dancing place. He had draft beer and music. Jim's parents, Jim's two sisters, Fred Kalhorn, and other friends had fun dancing and unwinding there. Jim, Fred, and I played tennis and golfed together and, of course, enjoyed beach parties.

Diving from South Haven south pier.

Chapter 4

Athletics

I was named after Jack Dempsey. My father grew up reading about and listening to the Jack Dempsey prize fights. Dempsey was the world heavyweight champion from 1919 to 1926, when he lost to Gene Tunney in the often-disputed match when the referee used a long count that ended up giving the championship to Tunney. Many people, including my father, thought that Dempsey should have been the winner of the fight. He always said that Jack Dempsey was the greatest of all heavyweight boxers. Later, while I was in the Navy, I met Jack Dempsey in New York City on Fifth Avenue, in front of his restaurant, where he was autographing postcards. I told him I was named after him, and he signed my card, "Your pal, Jack Dempsey."

My father and his five brothers all were good athletes. My uncle, Walter, was an all-state tackle. Notre Dame offered him a full scholarship, but he turned it down to stay in the family plumbing business. Later on, everyone in South Haven came to watch my father and uncle Walter in a boxing match. Uncle Walter won. In the mid-1930s the Fritz brothers' team won the South Haven basketball championship two years in a row. All of the brothers were tall. The rules then required a jump ball at half court after every basket was made. When I was four and five years old, I would run after basketballs that went out of bounds. The balls would go bumpity bump down the stairs that led to the locker rooms. I would scurry down the stairs and get the ball and throw it back to the players. When time outs were called, I would run, pick up the basketball, and try to shoot it toward the basket. Sometimes my father would hold me up so I could make the basket. My mother also was on a women's basketball team.

My mother's basketball team. She's on the far right.

The Fritz basketball team. My father is in the back row, center.

JACK FRITZ above, provides depth for the Rams at the guard spot, alternating with Chet Stefaniak, and Mickey Mohr. He has also seen some action as a forward.

Sophomore basketball at South Haven High School.

I really enjoyed basketball. The South Haven City Recreation Department had a Saturday basketball program for kids 12 and younger. I would eagerly trudge through the snow to the high school and play with the older kids. When I reached 13, I tried out for the seventh-grade basketball team. I guess I was a better player than the other seventh graders, so they moved me up to the eighth-grade team. The big game was at St. Joseph, MI. They traditionally were the best at basketball because, according to my father, their high school gym was open seven days a week. My freshman year, I played on the junior-varsity team most of the year and was elevated to the varsity for the state tournament. I played in all of the games. During my junior year in high school, we played St. Joseph at home, where I guarded their all-state center, knocking the ball away and making him miss shots. I finally fouled out, but I had held him to only one point! We won that game, but St. Joseph went on to win the state championship. My highest number of points that season was 27, playing against Allegan, MI.

Freshman football at South Haven High.

Football for me began in the ninth grade on the junior varsity team. We were playing Fennville, a small town in the country, with a team composed mainly of Native American Chippewas. Their playing field was a combination of a cow pasture and irregular lines. I was given a hand-off and ran quickly through the defense. It was an easy score—I thought—as I stopped after crossing what I believed was the goal line. Next thing I knew, all the Indians were throwing me to the ground! The pasture was so badly marked that my "near" touchdown was not to be! I eventually I got the nickname "Freight Train Fritz," because it usually took several players to bring me down!

Tom Slaughter, our previous high school football coach, was my first-year coach at Western Michigan University. I remember one game, in particular, when we were playing the penitentiary at Battle Creek, MI. The field was mainly crushed stone, and we ended up with lots of stones in our faces—but we still won!

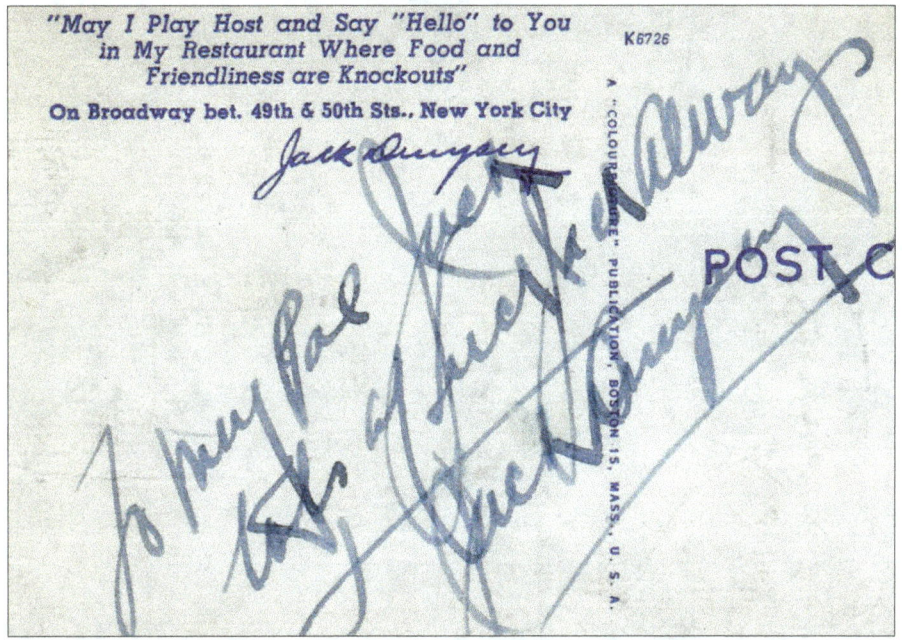

Postcard signed by Jack Dempsey, who I was named after.

Second Summer of lifeguarding, circa 1949.

Chapter 5

Work Ethic

When I was seven years old, my first memory of structured work was mowing our lawn on 602 Maple St. In order to move the lawnmower forward, I would grasp the handle and position myself at a 45-degree angle from the ground and push as hard as I could to get the blades rotating through the grass. Raking leaves in the Fall was the next big duty.

During the Winter, I would shovel the coal for the furnace through a window into the basement. Also I had to empty the ashes into a large metal wash tub and take them outside. And sometimes I would shovel the coal into the furnace.

World War II started when I was 10. My parents worked down the railroad tracks at the foundry and the aircraft-engine plant. My duties during the day were washing the dishes, cleaning the house, and taking care of the lawn. When these duties were done, I could then go to the beach or play pickup sports in the neighborhood. Almost every day I would open a can of tomato soup or Chef Boyardee spaghetti for lunch.

When I turned 13, my father told me that I would be working 20 hours a week for Mike Stimac at Food Town, a grocery/hamburger establishment across the street from the high school. During the war, my mother had worked with Mike at the defense plant. Every day after school, I walked across the street to work. The first thing I did was shovel the sidewalks. My other duties were as follows: refill the long pop case, sort the empty pop bottles into wooden containers, peel a 100-pound sack of potatoes, place each one onto the French fry slicer, make 50 pounds of hamburger patties, restock the grocery shelves, and scrub the floors.

On Saturdays, I washed all of the windows, made 150 pounds of hamburger patties, peeled 200 pounds of potatoes for French fries, filled the pop case, waited on customers, and scrubbed the floors—before I headed home for supper. I rode my bicycle about two miles to school every weekday. When I was playing football in the Fall and basketball in the Winter, I worked after practice. I took full advantage of study periods at school, since I had a tight work/study schedule. My fringe benefit was having a "Big Mike" and a chocolate milkshake for supper. During that first year, I grew six inches in height. I worked for 35 cents an hour and managed to save $3,000 after two years, which was a lot of money in those days!

My job at Food Town ended when my father started his own plumbing business and needed me as his helper. I was 15 at that time, and the job continued the next Summer, too. I worked 10-hour days, weekends included, for no salary. Every evening, I could consume a quart of milk at suppertime. During the Winter, I worked mostly Saturdays for my father. He had many customers from the Jewish resorts on the north side of South Haven. Often, I would ride my bicycle to these customers' homes or businesses and collect cash and checks, sometimes carrying several hundred dollars home. However, my mother and father weren't good at getting invoices out to customers, which eventually caused their business to end. My father was an extremely skilled master plumber who handled large projects very easily. But unfortunately, he didn't care for the business side of running his plumbing company.

In the Summer of 1957, my father felt sorry for having me work 60 hours a week for no pay and suggested I apply for a lifeguard job at the South Haven beach on Lake Michigan. I got the job, and we had two lifeguards at the North Beach and one at the South Beach, alternating every third week. Besides lifeguarding, we picked up debris from the lakeshores. We worked eight hours a day without an official break, unlike today, when lifeguards get breaks every 15 minutes.

Today few students work their way through college. Because I hadn't been paid to work for my parents' plumbing business, they paid for my tuition and books at Western Michigan. However, the first year and a half while in college, I worked at odd jobs like landscaping, unloading railroad cars, working at car washes, anything that I could find. Fortunately, I found a job at the Methodist church cleaning the nursery for the pastor's wife. She asked if I would like to clean her house on Saturdays, which I did. She told her neighbor, the pressroom supervisor for the *Kalamazoo Gazette*, about me, and he offered me a job on Saturday evening for the Sunday edition of the newspaper. I would arrive at the pressroom at 10 p.m. and wait for the papers to come off the press. My first duty was to load papers into an enclosure for the rural routes. That took two to three hours. At 2 a.m., I delivered large bundles of papers throughout Kalamazoo. Luckily, I had a radio in the van and listened to Randy's Record Shop, hearing the likes of Fats Domino, Louis Armstrong, and Elvis Presley.

Later on, I got more time at the newspaper, delivering "shorts and misses" to subscribers throughout Kalamazoo. My shift began at 3:30 p.m. and ended at 7:30 or 8. When no "misses" were called in, I could study in a small room at the newspaper. Because I had no car or bike, I walked two miles to the library, studied there, walked half a mile back to our apartment, studied again, and went to bed. The next day I attended classes, walked back to the *Kalamazoo Gazette*, and the process would begin all over again—seven days a week. My pay was 95 cents an hour. From this money, I contributed $5 a week for food and $20 a month for rent as my quarter-share in the apartment arrangement.

Football sweater at Western Michigan University.

Chapter 6

Education

WHEN I WAS 10 AND 11 YEARS OLD, I would spend two weeks each Summer at my Aunt Do's home in Chicago. Her late husband was an author and her library was full of great books. I spent most of my time there reading Mark Twain novels and several adult novels and short stories. Aunt Do encouraged me to someday go to college. She was a very important influence in my life. Uncle Harold told me to get as much math in school as possible, so I took algebra one and two-plus trigonometry. I also took physics and Latin in high school.

In 1939, I started grade school at the Indiana Avenue Grade School, built in 1875. My father had completed classes there, beginning in 1916 from grades four to eight. In the Fall of 1947, I transferred to Central Grade School. My teacher was excellent; she used lots of participative-learning exercises, and I excelled in her spelling bees. As the school year proceeded, I noticed that she was gaining weight in her mid-section, and later on that Spring, another teacher took her place. We found out she had a baby boy! Occasionally, we were led down the hallway to the high school auditorium to enjoy orchestra and band concerts. Mr. Listieartch was the high school band teacher. Almost every year, the South Haven High School band won first place in the statewide competition. During August, the band would assemble outside of the high school and parade through the streets of South Haven. We could hear the band several blocks away, and we would run to watch them march and play their instruments.

As early infants, boys were given rudimentary toys that simulated actual adult building tools. There were peg-pounding boards, tinker toys, and erector sets. Whittling wood with a jackknife with leftover wood afforded all sorts of creative forms—making boats, animals, and other things. We also used cards to fabricate miniature rooms, stacking one room atop another until the entire structure collapsed. We also observed actual construction in the neighborhood.

One day, a boy named Ruddy and I had a fight at recess. He was a bully who liked to antagonize my classmates into fights, which he normally would win. Once, he challenged me during recess and began wrestling with me, but I took him down and forced his arm behind his back. We went rolling down a grassy slope, and I pinned him to the ground again. He screamed out at Mr. Slaughter for help. Mr. Slaughter was the high school football, basketball, and track coach, and he knew that Ruddy was a bully. He just stood back and watched until Ruddy gave up. There were no more problems after that!

In 1947, I was elected president of my class. Our teacher, Miss Hildebrand caught Dick Collins chewing gum in class. It was one of several rules that she strictly enforced. She decided to stage a mock trial, hopefully to convict Dick of his alleged offense. A jury of myself and five others was chosen. Paul Gaston was selected as the attorney to defend Dick. Another student was chosen as the prosecutor. I was the moderator of the jury. I asked if anyone actually had seen Dick chew the gum? No one had. We concluded that there was insufficient evidence to try Dick. Paul Gaston brought forth the findings of the jury. The teacher asked for the verdict of our jury and the charge against Dick was dismissed. Miss Hildebrand, a strict disciplinarian, was quite upset. Paul graduated from the University of Michigan and became an outstanding lawyer and, later, chief counsel for the Brunswick Corporation. Regardless of the outcome of this incident, I admired Miss Hildebrand more than any teacher I ever had. She expected a lot from us, and we learned a lot from her.

Sometimes in high school during lunch breaks, we would cross the street to Louie Hoffman's little store to buy treats. Louie had a slight stutter and, after we paid him, he would reply, "Tank yu." I still imitate his cute way of speaking many years later.

In 1952, I entered Western Michigan University in Kalamazoo. My mother was very excited—especially because none of her family ever had a college degree. She wanted me to dress like a '20s Ivy League student and bought me a heavy, full-length coat that reached all the way down to my shoes. During orientation, I talked to several girls, and I don't think the coat helped in getting dates with them. I wore the coat the first day of classes and that was enough; I never wore it again. Of course, it was September and fairly warm outside. When it got colder, I went to the Western Michigan Surplus store and bought a tanker coat, which was in style at the college in those days.

My first semester began with an elective course called "Man and Society," as well as required classes in Engineering Drawing and Calculus. I guess that I thought that engineering would be a good profession. It wasn't very long into the calculus class that I became lost and was falling behind. I wasn't doing very well in Man and Society either. Quite a few others were in the same boat. The instructor, Sam Clark, got us all together and showed us how to study in college, and it got a bit easier for us after that.

Another course, English One was fun. The professor was very friendly to everyone, and we would meet him in one of the rooms at the dorm, where he also lived. He was from a ranch in Wyoming. It was fun writing essays for his class as he enjoyed my hunting and fishing stories. I also had a Beginning Speech course, and I was the only boy in the class. Our professor was Miss Lindbloom. Every time I got up to give a speech, she would tear me to shreds. She never gave me any constructive advice on how to improve. Unfortunately, I failed the course, which didn't get me off to a very good start in college. I later took the class over with another instructor, who was young and attractive, and got a B!

Unfortunately, again for me, my father wanted me to spend some weekends back in South Haven helping him in his plumbing business. One weekend that I came home was during mid-term exams, which took a toll on my grades. During my first semester, I was on the freshman football team, which also reduced the time I had to study. All told, I had one B, mostly Cs and the one F.

Varsity football at Western Michigan University.

My sophomore year in college, I played on the varsity football team. During practice, I suffered a severe concussion and spent a week in the infirmary. One of my girlfriends brought my lessons to me so that I could keep up with my studies. After several medical tests, my doctor suggested that I stop playing football. Since I'd already had a concussion playing football in high school, I decided it was a good thing to do. It also gave me ample time to study. And getting the job at the Kalamazoo Gazette allowed me to study between delivering newspapers and shorts. The job also helped me to become more mature and independent.

In class, I enjoyed my courses, especially Industrial Psychology, which led to choosing Psychology as my major. I also liked writing, so I decided to minor in English. My eight hours in Labor Relations were enjoyable, too, along with other courses such as Business Cycles. So I decided to choose Economics as my second minor. I also had to take biology, chemistry, statistics, and additional math courses to obtain my Bachelor of Science degree in General Studies.

My friends and I would go for coffee at the Student Union, where we chatted and had coffee with many other students. The first college dance was upcoming, so my high school friend, Fred Kalhorn, and I double-dated with two nice girls. We later asked them if they wanted to go to the city's toboggan park. The runs were at a very steep 45-degree angle. It was fun riding backwards down the 100 yards to the bottom. In October, I asked a nice girl to go the Fall dance. I had planned to hitchhike home, hunt pheasants, and drive back to the dance that evening. Unfortunately, no one gave me a ride, so I walked home and then went hunting for the rest of the day. I was so exhausted that I couldn't drive back for the dance that night. I called my date and said I wouldn't be able to take her to the dance. Needless to say, I had a hard time getting dates for a long time after that!

My other high school friend, Jim Morris, and I used fake IDs to get into a nightclub downtown. One weekend, I had my parent's car. We met two girls at the club and took them for a ride. We all were smoking cigarettes, and the lighted end of a cigarette burned the passsenger seat of the car. I thought I'd really get chewed out by my father, but luckily he didn't say anything!

During the Summer months, my friends and I would have frequent beach parties just outside of town. At this point, I want to explain how one of my girlfriends and I, while sitting in my parents' car, observed a strange phenomenon. Rita Held, one of my summertime girlfriends and I were parked on a high bluff overlooking Lake Michigan. Bright stars covered the sky, and the moon was about to come up. Suddenly, far out on the horizon about 20 miles away, a bright, dot-sized figure appeared. It traveled at an immense speed and was a brighter white than any object I'd ever seen. We were sure it was a UFO and felt fortunate not to have been kidnapped! It swept by the bluff and disappeared over Lake Michigan. This was in 1955, when UFO sightings were reported in many parts of the United States.

Fridays after classes were over, we would all go downtown to the beer hall where all the college students hung out. We never had dinner, as the common saying was "beer is food!" But when we did eat, we had a favorite tavern where we would devour deep-fried smelt—heads, guts, and all!

The second semester of my sophomore year, I moved from the dorm to an upstairs apartment on Steward Avenue. It was an old, Victorian-style house that had been converted into apartments. My friend, Fred Kalhorn, myself, and two other guys shared the $80 a month rent. And we had a big coffee can that held the $5 we each placed in there weekly to buy food. By Friday, the can would be nearly empty. Sometimes, I would bring back from home large steaks from moose hunted by my dad.

We sometimes would arrange parties on Friday nights. Usually, we never knew which four girls we'd pair up with. The way we figured it out was intriguing. Charlie had a tape recorder, and we would hide it behind the davenport and start it up. When the girls got there, we'd tell them we were going to buy the beer. When we got back, we'd hustle the girls into the kitchen and replay the tape to find out who they preferred as their dates. The next day we'd play back the noisy party sounds, too.

On my way to class at Western Michigan University.

Having an apartment three miles from campus and a job—without a car or even a bike—really had its challenges. A lot of times on my walk home from studying at the library, I would stop by the city fountain that had colored, dancing water. I would sit for a long time, mesmerized by it. It was great therapy!

In the Summer of 1954, I returned to South Haven to work for my father's plumbing company. Jim Morris was home on leave from the Air Force, and we spent time together looking for pretty maidens and attending parties. One evening, Jim and I took two girls for a boat ride. I was in the backseat with my date when Jim revved up the boat and water came splashing on us, as he turned and swerved between the rolling waves. Later that evening, we built a beach fire and enjoyed the gentle waves rolling onto the shore. My date was Margaret Edmonton, a junior at Indiana University, where her father was an astrology professor. She was a waitress at Mendelsons resort, and I dated her most of that Summer.

Later that Summer, my best friend, Fred Kalhorn, and I headed west in his '48 Chevy convertible. I had never been more than 400 miles away from home. I was very excited after crossing the plains on Route 66 and seeing the Rocky Mountains appear on the horizon. We drove through Denver then south to the Rocky Mountain State Park and up to Grand Lake, where we rented a room in an old rundown building. We heard mice running across the ceiling, but that didn't bother us.

With Fred Kalhorn, at right, on our road trip to California.

The next morning was beautiful, so we decided to rent horses and ride four miles to a waterfall. We asked for the gentlest horses they had, since we were inexperienced riders. We rode about two miles and stopped to rest. A trail ahead led off the main trail to the right. Not seeing any signs for the waterfall, we decided to continue straight ahead. The horses did not want to go, so we prodded them along. Unbeknown to us, we were headed upward toward the top of Pike's Peak. We had brought no water or food. We continued through beautiful mountain lakes and passed under boulders and stopped for water in the lakes. It was past noon when we decided we should head back down the mountain. The horses were so good as they would stop to figure how to slide down the larger rock formations. By the time we finally neared the town, it was almost dark. All of a sudden, both horses bolted and ran full speed into town and into the barn, while we hung on for dear life! It was like a scene from an old Western movie. The horses had earned their dinners that night!

After getting a good night's rest in the same mouse-infested building, we hit the road and drove day and night, sleeping in the car. Finally, we reached Vandenberg Air Force Base in Lompoc, CA, where our buddy, Jim Morris, was stationed. We hadn't eaten much for the past two days, so Jim got some Air Force uniforms for us and we went through the chow line with him. Next day, eight of us drove to Yosemite National Park. We watched the fire fall from the top of the mountain, as a woman sang the Indian Love Song. Later, we had a party at the El Capitan campground. Several girls came but departed after we'd had one too many drinks. We then drove back to the main center and slept under some giant redwood trees.

With Jim Morris, at right, in my borrowed Air Force uniform.

The next morning, I woke up around 9 o'clock to a beautiful, sunny day. The first thing I heard was Jim saying, "Does anyone want to go to the church with me?" I said I would go with him. We had to hurry because the mass was just getting started. We noticed that most of the seats already were taken. Jim managed to get a seat on the right side of the church, and a man slid over to make room for me, so I was sitting right on the aisle. Since the service was all in Latin, I really didn't know what to do, so I kept watching the gentleman next to me. When he kneeled, I quickly kneeled; when he did the sign of the cross up-down and sideways, I hurriedly did the same. I mimicked all the prayers as best that I could. After a while, I noticed two men on the far side of the church grasping poles with nets attached, and behind me another man had pole and net. All of a sudden, the man next to me began shoving me into the aisle, saying, "Hurry, they need you!" At that moment, the other attendant handed me an offering pole. I watched as the two on the opposite side began walking forward, so I followed behind my partner. I had the outside section where Jim was seated. I followed and turned to the front of the congregation and kneeled before the priest, always watching my partners and imitating everything they did. I walked to my side of the church and paused at every row. As I was nearing Jim's row, I looked right over him, keeping a serious countenance. We then took the offerings back to the priest. As I returned to my seat, I looked at Jim and he was laughing so hard that there were tears in his eyes. After the service, he said, "I've been a Catholic all of my life; I've been a candle lighter and an altar boy but never did take the offering. The first time in the church for you, and you got to take the offering!" (Another interesting religious experience was when I had an audience with Pope Pius. See Chapter 7 – U.S. Navy.) By the time we returned to the air base, we had little time to get back to Michigan and the university for the Fall semester.

One Friday night, I had finished delivering newspapers at 2:30 a.m. for the *Kalamazoo Gazette*. There was a fierce storm outside, so I slept in a storage area near the office. The next morning, I finally arrived at my apartment about 8:30. There I met this beautiful dark-haired, blue-eyed gal. She had been waiting all night for me! I never did get a date with her. Oh well, that's the breaks you get or don't get in life. The South Haven girls that we all knew were good friends. Sometimes they would come and bring Michigan State University girls or others for social get-togethers. During my junior and senior years, the partying dropped off substantially. I attended Summer classes before my senior year so I would be able to graduate the following Spring. Most of the time was spent working and studying.

In June of 1956, we were to graduate. Fred Kalhorn and I woke up to a beautiful, sunshiny day. All the graduates donned their caps and gowns outside the football stadium. My mother, father, and grandmother Fritz sat in the stands and watched as I received my Bachelor of Science degree. Afterward, we all drove to our apartment and enjoyed a nice lunch. Those four years built a solid platform for future accomplishments.

ESSAYS

I WAS NINE YEARS OLD and in middle school when my uncle Harold was drafted into the Army. At first, my reason for writing was that I felt sorry for his wife and baby girl being left by themselves. Later, I was excited about the fighting. After my uncle fought in the Battle of the Bulge, he crossed the Rhine River into Germany. Because my grandparents immigrated from Germany around 1878, I asked my uncle to "send me some German dirt." It caused a wave of laughter from the other soldiers. I do believe that these letters, written at an early age, gave me practice and experience for later in life. The following essays will give you a glimpse into my literary efforts in middle and high school.

'AN EVENING OF BIRD HUNTING'

"THERE ARE SOME PEOPLE WHO DON'T LIKE TO HUNT. Most of these people have never experienced the beauty and fragrance of the outdoors. They have never thrilled while watching a beautiful bird dog as she whisks through a large open field or through a small bogie swale. They have never seen the excitement in her body as she jumps on a hot track. The fun and enjoyment of hunting can never be forgotten.

"The sun was shining just above the treetops. There was a freshness in the air as the wind gently ruffled the long, grown clover. It was a perfect evening for hunting. My father and I had just parked our Model-A car next to a wide open clover field. 'This place looks good,' he said as he reached in his pocket and deposited three shells into his 1897 Winchester pump gun. 'It sure is, right next to that cornfield,' I replied. I opened the trunk and out jumped Ginger, our Irish Setter. In her hurry to get out, she almost knocked me over. She quickly jumped over the ditch and wiggled under the fence. I loaded my gun and followed Dad into the field. We spread out about 30 yards from each other and slowly started to walk across the field. Ginger was circling in front of us, covering every foot of the ground. As I walked along, I noticed padded-down grass and clover where pheasants had been roosting. 'There are some good signs here,' I shouted to Dad. 'I know, I've seen them,' he replied.

Dagmar, one of our hunting dogs.

"Pretty soon we reached the end of the field. It was here that we began watching Ginger closely. She had hit a track. Her small body moved excitedly as she snuck through the grass. Back and forth she ran, trying to pick up the hottest track. Finally, she hit it, and as she drew closer to the bird, she took bounding leaps, trying to make the bird fly. One more leap and up he went. There was a thundering of wings as a big cock jumped and flew into the air. Both guns cracked as the bird flew out of the field over a ravine and up above some trees on the side. 'I didn't expect him to get up so soon,' said Dad. 'I had my back toward him when he got up and had to take a long shot,' I replied. Ginger was really excited now, for she had heard the sound of the guns.

"'Where shall we go now?' I asked Dad. 'Let's try that wheat field on the other side of the ravine and then work toward those trees. We may be able to jump him again.' 'OK,' I said. With that we started down the slightly sloping hill into the ravine; at the bottom we came to a swale with a few trees spread through it. We watched Ginger as she circled the swale. She showed no signs of excitement, so we walked up the other slope and climbed over a barbed-wire fence at the top. Starting here, we worked along the edge of the wheat field. Halfway down the field, Ginger hit another track. She ran back and forth along the side of the field. She jumped from the field and ran into a small grouping of trees, but here she lost the track. 'He must have run into the woods and flown. We'll hunt on the other side of the woods and maybe we'll pick up his track,' said Dad. After walking through the moss-covered woods, we emerged into a small patch of sharp, prickly briars. At one side of the briar patch, we saw a hunter with his dog. He had a little black-and-white cocker spaniel. 'Any luck?' I yelled. 'Yep, just jumped one on the other side of the road. He was over in that apple orchard and I think he flew over here somewhere. Did you get anything yet?' 'We jumped one but missed him,' I replied. After talking for a few minutes we proceeded on our way.

"Soon we reached a small, wooded area. Between the trees, there was some knee-high marsh grass growing. The ground here was slightly damp. Ginger pushed her way through the thick grass and kept her nose to the damp ground. Finally, she began to vigorously wag her tail. With one quick motion, she was on her way, moving through the grass. As she drew nearer her prey, she slowed up and sneaked slowly through the grass like a tiger. Then she stopped and came to a dead point. She looked beautiful with her head cocked and her ears perked up. She took a few steps more and stopped again. This time we were ready. I was on one side of the trees and Dad was on the other side. 'Flush 'em,' Dad said to Ginger. With two quick jumps, she put up the pheasant. It was a beautiful sight as the big cock leaped into the air. Dad had the best position on the bird, so I let him have the shot. The second his gun cracked, the bird folded up and hit the ground. What a shot, I thought as I ran over and picked up the pheasant. I let Ginger smell him and then put him in the back of Dad's hunting jacket. Dad ejected his shell and put in a new one.

"'Let's try that wheat field next to the corn,' I said. 'Last week, Pat and I flushed a big cock there.' We walked out of the small wooded area, across a clover field and on into the wheat fields. We jumped two hens but nothing more. The sun was setting low in the western sky now, and the red rays reflected on the fields around us. Soon, we came to a little swale just below a low, rolling hill. Near the edge of the swale, Ginger picked up a track. She ran back and forth through the thick grass. Then, just two feet from me, the bird jumped into the air. Out over the open field he flew. I gave him about a foot and shot. He folded up and tumbled to the ground. 'Good shot,' Dad yelled. We put him in Dad's jacket and we started back to the car. Everything seemed good now as we walked up the bare, sloping field. The sun had just set, and the sky was a beautiful red, with pink clouds running through it. It was truly an end of a perfect evening of hunting."

'FIRST DEER-HUNTING TRIP'

"It was just four o'clock in the morning when we rolled into Charlevoix, MI. Bob Ketner, my father Harry, my uncle Harold, and I had just driven 300 miles in one night. The weather was somewhat cold, with no snow, until we arrived at Reed City, where the snow was a foot deep. When we finally got to Cadillac, a raging blizzard had begun. When we finally got to Charlevoix, the storm had passed. We slept in a boarding house until 7 a.m., when the alarm clock woke us up. We dressed in a hurry and walked downtown, where we saw the ferry boat waiting. The boat held four cars, 30 passengers, and a ton of luggage. This was the boat that we were to take to Beaver Island. I had sailed on it before, and got plenty sick before the four-hour crossing was over. The boat didn't leave until 8 a.m., so we went down to the restaurant for a cup of coffee. It was there we found out that Lake Michigan was rolling with white caps. So we decided to fly across the lake, rather than to get seasick. We saw three of the Olson brothers at the restaurant and talked about how hunting would be. The year before, the six brothers all got their bucks in two days. After leaving the restaurant, we went down to the boat dock and started loading our things. After doing this, we went up to a drugstore and called the airport. The pilot there said he would take the plane up and see how the weather was. After going up, he said the weather was fine and he would take us across.

My first deer!

"As we left town for the airport, we could hear the boat's whistle as it steamed out of the harbor. Having arrived at the airport, the pilot took us out to the plane. Only my father, my uncle, and I were going across first. Our friend Bob was to fly with the two Olson brothers later. The pilot warmed up the motor of his Stinson and taxied to the end of the field. The engine started to roar louder and louder, and before we knew it, we were in the air. As we flew over Lake Michigan, we could see the Mary Margaret steaming out of the harbor. Far off to the west, we could see Beaver Island, where I was soon to get the joy of a lifetime. As I watched the waves below, I was glad I was flying instead of leaning over the side of the Mary Margaret. In 15 minutes, we were flying over St. James, the only town on Beaver Island. We circled the town two times and then headed for the airport, which was located five miles west of St. James. As we flew over the island, we could see the many lakes, the large, open clearings, the huge, hardwood forests and the thick, open swamps, where soon all the deer would be driven by the sounds of guns. We could see the whole island, which is 80 miles in circumference. The pilot checked the wind and found out that we could land in a large open field, just outside of town. We glided to a perfect landing on the snow-covered field. The plane stopped and we stepped out. The plane took off, and we headed for town. We hadn't walked far down the road when a car from town stopped and picked us up. We drove around some curves and soon were in St. James. The town had a few Indians, but most of the people were Irish. We stopped by to see Gus Mithie, the road commissioner. He had provided us with a small tractor shack on the east side of the island. When the boat came in a little later, we unloaded our luggage into one of Gus's trucks and carried it out to the shack. It took us most of the afternoon to get settled. Bob and I worked, while Harold and my dad went out scouting the territory. We had seen tracks running through this place. The deer would come out of the woods into the clearing and down to the lake to drink.

"When Dad and Harold came back, Bob and I had supplies ready. All during dealing with the supplies, we talked about the next day. Dad picked a place for me right in the middle of a highway that had never been completed. We had seen tracks running through this place. The deer would come out of the woods, into the highway clearing over the road, and down to the lake to drink. Dad, Harold, and Bob would all go into the woods to hunt. After making our plans, we all hit the sack.

"The following morning, the alarm went off at 5 o'clock. Dad lit the Coleman lantern, we dressed, and ate breakfast. Plans were made for me to stand under a tree on the edge of the clearing, about 100 yards from where the deer tracks were found. Dad reminded me to stay as still as possible while scanning the clearing and to stay under the small tree where the deer could not see me. He then disappeared into the woods. The sky was overcast, with gray clouds and temperatures below freezing. My feet and hands were cold, but I remained still, slowly scanning the clearing. All at once, there was a spotted movement downhill, near the edge of the clearing. An eight-point, white-tailed deer stepped out into the clearing. I unlocked my 30/30 Winchester rifle and aimed at the buck. He picked up the pace quickly, and I had to respond accordingly. The rifle cracked off with a deafening roar, and the deer dropped to the ground. My heart pumped with excitement, and I ran down to where the deer was lying. The bullet had passed through the jugular vein in his neck, killing him instantly. After about 45 minutes, Dad appeared and I said, 'Dad, I got him!' Then he asked all kinds of questions. He finished gutting him and laid him up against a stump and I helped dressing him out. That evening, we went to the tavern in town and celebrated my first deer hunt. Dad wanted me to get back to South Haven quickly so that I wouldn't miss much school. So he put me on the airplane and I landed in Charlevoix. I then hitchhiked 200 miles to South Haven. Next day in the Hi-Wi Club class, I gave my first presentation to the class!"

HIGH SCHOOL ESSAYS

'Integration of Races'
"In the early 1950s, racial discrimination was creeping back into place. My 11th-grade teacher asked us to write something about this topic. At the same time, my mother belonged to a book club where

they were reviewing classic plays. I have always had imaginative ideas and/or unique solutions to various situations. I thought about writing something that might influence positive changes where all races could work toward eliminating discrimination. I thought about it for a while and decided that I would write a play. I wanted to envision what the world would be like 300 years out.

"The first scene showed what the architecture would look like. Inside, a history teacher explained why everyone looked the same. He said that through the hundreds of years, wars and social changes had led to multiple interracial marriages, which eventually made everyone almost the same."

It is ironic to see how the process has begun to take shape 70 years later. My teacher was quite impressed and gave me an A+. It fits right in now with the "Black Lives Matter" movement that is causing drastic changes in society.

'Lake Michigan Water Fluctuations'

The following year I completed a term paper on fluctuations in Lake Michigan water levels. The paper included charts dating back to the past century. At the time I wrote the paper, the lake was at its lowest level, but as I write this book, it's at its highest level, due to global warming.

'Trigonometry Project'

In 1952, I built a manipulative, educational aide for trigonometry class. It consisted of three metal disks that slid to different lengths as they circled around a grooved, wooden disk. Different angles and lengths of the three sides of a triangle were used by the teacher in addressing the functional relationships and formulas used to acquire the results of various equations.

Drawing I made in school of our cottage on the shore of Lake Michigan.

With two cute children in Valencia, Spain.

Chapter 7

The United States Navy

After graduating from Western Michigan, I returned to South Haven and began preparing for a job in the personnel field. I prepared a resume and cover letter and tried to get into the Whirlpool Corporation in Benton Harbor, MI. Most of the openings there were in the engineering field. I drove to Chicago and met a wonderful lady who had an employment agency. She sent me to Campbell Soups, Revlon, and other companies. I did get an offer from UPS, but didn't want to begin my career driving trucks. In the meantime, I worked with my dad. The next trip to Chicago, after several job interviews, I became frustrated. One day, I passed a U.S. Navy recruiting office and thought maybe I would apply for the Officer Training School in Rhode Island. I took the test and passed it.

In October of 1956, I took a train to the U.S. Navy Training Center in Newport, RI. The initial training was compressed into an eight-week program. We went to class every day, and I was very interested in all of the courses, especially refrigeration. Marching and small-arms drills were held between classes. Our company commander was a Navy pilot and learning to become one was the primary purpose of the program. We only studied one day of navigation in the entire eight weeks. We were lectured extensively on "three-point sightings on charts" to establish a direct route through middle-channel plots. Near the end of the program, we all were fitted for our officer's uniform.

Unfortunately, I was informed that I was not selected. They were looking for pilots, and I probably didn't pass the navigation course. I think that I would have made it through the program successfully if we'd had more hands-on assistance from the instructors.

At the time, I felt badly, but there were several others who didn't make it either, and we all wanted to get to OCS boot camp. Upon completion of the OCS program, we were obligated to three years of active duty. If we didn't complete that program (which I didn't), we were required to enlist for a two-year period. I felt fortunate to have served the two years for my country.

I next was sent to Baltimore, MD, where it was cold and there was lots of snow. I clearly remember how we had to stand outside in the cold for long periods of time, waiting to get into the cafeteria. We'd be awakened at 2 a.m. to scrub floors! Our company had a swim meet, and I helped them win. As a reward, I was assigned to military police duty in downtown Baltimore. I had my Elks Club card and spent time going in for a drink.

Later, I was sent to a center to wait for an assignment—either land-based or shipboard. I wanted land-based duty, but—just like the military—I was assigned to the USS Randolph CV15, an attack carrier that patrolled the Northeast Atlantic and Mediterranean. The ship was berthed in New York City, and I walked up the gang plank and reported for duty. I was assigned to the Operations Division in the Air Intelligence section. My rating was yeoman and my duties were to maintain and update target folders, maps, and classified information. Most of the work was done in a large briefing room in the middle of the ship. We referred to it as the Air Intelligence Office. Lt. Robert Reece was the commanding office of our section, and Lt. Robert Erwin was second in command. They were very congenial and welcomed me aboard. I learned that the Randolph had earned the "Battle E Award" as the best attack-aircraft carrier in the U.S. Navy for the third straight year.

Later that week, we had an all-hands party in a nearby building. It was a chance for us to become acquainted with Capt. Smith, the ship's commanding officer. We entered the building and noticed that, up on the stage, there were 10 kegs of beer. The room was filled to capacity. Pitchers of beer were placed on tables all around the hall. Soon, the tall, good-looking Capt. Smith, or "Smitty," as he was nicknamed, approached the microphone and expressed his appreciation to the crew for its hard work and dedication. He then held up his mug of beer and said, "We've got the best damn ship in the whole Navy," whereupon the hall exploded in cheers. Later, I learned that Capt. Smith gave lots of liberty (time-off) when we were ashore. The crew appreciated it and worked diligently for him. Following are journals I wrote while serving my two years. They give a detailed account of everyday activities, both at sea and ashore.

NAVAL JOURNALS

"For the next seven months, the Randolph will be part of the U.S. Sixth Fleet, operating in Mediterranean waters. As a major unit of that fleet, we carry very real responsibilities in supporting America's foreign policy of preserving the security of both the United States and the free countries whose lifelines depend on freedom of movement in the Mediterranean. We must be ready to act quickly whenever this security is jeopardized.

"Twice, during the last six months, two incidents have occurred that showed the Sixth Fleet's ability to carry out its basic job of keeping the peace. During the Suez crisis last November, the Sixth Fleet was responsible for the evacuation of more than 2,000 American citizens who were trapped in that war zone. Additionally, the Sixth Fleet's position and strength were highly effective in preventing spread of the Suez fight and had a strong enforcement effect in support of United Nations resolutions. Less than six months later, our fleet again was called upon to show its strength to prevent hostile powers from intervening in the Jordanian crisis. These demonstrations quelled situations that possibly could have resulted in a third world war. It's important for us to realize that the mobility and dispersion capabilities inherent in the carrier task force have given the Sixth Fleet the frontline position in our defensive structure.

"You will be interested to know that, not only was the Sixth Fleet in position to figure heavily in the successful outcome of the Suez crisis, but also additional forces were deployed that more than doubled the strength of the Sixth Fleet. Characteristically, this was done 'overnight.'

"Russian submarines, destroyers, and cruisers, are flexing their muscles in the Mediterranean, and it will be the striking power of our fleet that prevents them from throwing any punches. Our cruise with the Sixth Fleet will be more than just a training cruise; it will be a working cruise. We will be working to guard our country and our way of life. So as we enjoy the pleasures of our Mediterranean ports of call, remember that ours is an important role in a highly important effort."

MAY 4, 1957
"We just pulled into Mayport (FL) Naval Air Station this morning. We're leaving again this afternoon and will be in Norfolk on Monday. Last night I saw 'The Seven Year Itch' for the second time. After the movie, I walked out onto the flight deck and watched an electrical storm that we had just passed through. It was a beautiful picture because we were sailing through a clear area of moonlight and stars, and off on the horizon, lightning lit the sky like a neon sign through the clouds.

"Last weekend, we went to Virginia Beach. It's a lot like Jacksonville Beach, except that there are no bars or arcades along the sea walk. It's more like the north side of South Haven. Most of the houses are old and have been transformed into resorts. The seawall extends for about four miles. The ocean is cleaner than in Florida and about 10 degrees cooler. I've picked up a pretty good tan for only two days on the beach. After getting back on the ship, I went up on the flight deck for three more hours of sunbathing. The holiday routine starts just after lunch on Saturday. We were shown some pictures on venereal disease this morning. Somehow, the air conditioning got turned off here in the office and it's hot! Tonight, I'm going to a Western movie, which is shown on the hangar deck.

"It's Sunday morning now, and there is no unnecessary work done Sunday mornings. The movie last night was in technicolor, and it was very good. After the movie, we hit some strong winds and high seas. It seemed like we were rocking around in a roller coaster!

"I am putting in for 11 days of leave, commencing June 18 and ending June 30. The ship will be in Norfolk on May 28, so I'll go home from there. I will have to meet the ship at Mayport on June 30. The next day we leave for the Mediterranean and will be over there for eight months.

"Tomorrow night, I'm on a work party unloading ammunition. I've been pretty lucky about extra details. Sometimes while on board, everyone has to work down in the galley. Believe me, I'm staying away from that place for as long as I can. All the planes have been flown to Mayport and left there."

July 3, 1957

"Thus far, the weather has been wonderful for the Atlantic crossing. After three days, the sky has been a constant blue, with the sun and breeze never ceasing. I spent time this morning exploring the ship. Toward the rear of the ship, the crews were painting the motorboats that soon would be seeing more than their share of duty. Their brushes expertly stroked the green paint onto the bottoms of the slender keels. This part of the ship offered a constant intermingling of noise. From the port side came the hammering of the body fitters, while above the fantail, the humming of busy saws could be heard from the wood shop. On my way back, the crew was moving a large AD 'Sky Warrior' jet airplane toward the starboard elevator. Each massive blade of the propeller extended out a full 14 feet. It's hard to imagine that a single-engine plane of this type can haul as much as the B17s of World War II could. They truthfully are called the 'workhorse' of the Navy. A large blast from the safetyman's whistle brought the AD to a halt on the elevator. A bell rang out and, instantly, 6,000 tons of elevator rose to the flight deck.

"After climbing up 10 decks of winding ladders, I found myself on the 07 level, which is the uppermost deck on the carrier's island. This level is primarily used for watch-standers and observers. The stern-most section offers the best view of the landings and is where movies of each plane are recorded, in case of an accident. Below, on the flight deck, the red, yellow, blue, and orange uniforms of the airmen show brilliantly in the sun. The bright-yellow towing cars scurried along the deck, clearing the catapults and runway. From the bridge came the order for the ADs to start their engines. The AD engines started with popping and a bellow of orange flame. As the order is given to start the jets, the ship makes a heel to port, leaving a sickle-like wave behind her stern. The jet engines grew from a whistle to a thundering roar. The combinations of both types of planes caused the steel plating on the bridge to vibrate, and it forced small rivulets of water from the side of the ship.

USS Randolph attack carrier.

"Soon, noise from the 40 plane engines was roaring across the deck, the blades from the ADs casting reflections from the sun. Two sleek, gray Furies quickly moved onto the two forward catapults. Steel barriers slid up from inside the deck directly behind the jets' tails to divert the blast. The engines increased in intensity until you could feel the vibration throughout your body. Waves of hot air flowed back to the bridge, then, suddenly, the starboard catapult let loose, thrusting the plane across the deck and into the sky. The other planes followed in quick succession. Immediately after the last jet was launched, the next AD revved its engines to a peak and thundered off the runway into the sky.

"The whole deck suddenly cleared and was now ready for landings. Above the ship, several planes flew in tight formation, first appearing as specks and gradually taking shape, before streaking overhead with a solid blast. ADs hovered overhead, their engines humming in smooth, mellow drones. Then, the jets formations began circling the ship in steady waves. Now, the first jet was given the signal to land. Far out, off the starboard bow, moving against the motion of the ship, the jet moves in for its approach, while on board a wind of 40 miles an hour pushed across the deck. One mile out, and behind the starboard quarter, the jet begins to bank, making a full, 180-degree turn. It straightens out and then follows a path directly over the wake of the ship. Now, the jet is about 1,000 feet from the ship, wing flaps, air brakes, and landing gear down, dropping at a rate of 30 feet per second. Despite the effects of these braking apparatuses, the plane still is descending at 130 mph; it looks like a seagull gliding onto a perch. As the pilot lowers the stabilizer, the jet makes its final descent. The tailhook grabs the steel cable, and the jet screeches to an abrupt halt, landing a mere 80 feet from the stern. Three airmen rush to the trapped creature and release the cable. As the hook is released, the wings slowly ascend and the jet quickly moves forward and clear of the landing path. Thirty seconds later, another Fury screeches to a halt. Within six minutes, all of the jets are landed. The prop plane came in much the same but was stopped with much more grace and ease. One lone, two-engine AD ends the operation, as her huge structure lands with a boom, her hydraulic landing gear giving with the impact.

"The rest of the afternoon, I spent sorting TISs (Target Information Sheets). After supper, I still had some extra work to do. My job consisted of reassembling the shelves in the vault. Then I spent two hours recapping today's activities. At 2200 hours, it was ordered that all clocks be moved ahead by one hour, conforming with the new time zone. Over the squawk box came the boatswains mate's whistle and the usual announcement: 'Taps, taps, lights out, lights out.' The smoking lamp is out throughout the ship. Pause, then silence. The evening prayer is given by the chaplain. I settled comfortably into my bunk and bid farewell to another day at sea."

JULY 4, 1957
"Most of the morning was spent in the berthing compartment awaiting the call for our laundry. At 10, my section reported to the after-mess deck, where we were lectured on conduct ashore by the medical officer, shore-patrol officer, and the chaplain. The lecture covered such things as customs of the local people, where to go, what to buy, what not to talk about, etc. The 'tours offered' was covered quite vividly by the chaplain.

"One hour prior to lunch was spent inventorying TISs. Lunch consisted of pork chops, beans, potatoes, and cake. After lunch, Thomas and I shot a couple of pictures on the flight deck. The weather was very pleasant. Large masses of haze clouded the sky, with just enough space to allow the sun to shine through. From the flight deck, we could see the tanker, USS Canisteo, on the starboard side. Several rubber fueling lines weaved their way like roller coasters between the ships, rising and lowering with the pitch of the ships. A destroyer cut its way to the other side and also took on fuel. All three of the gray creatures maintained identical speeds as they moved up and down with the rolling sea.

"I spent most of the evening listening to records here in the office. At 2100, I took a walk up on the flight deck. There was a half moon in the western sky, which mirrored its silvery beams across the wide expanse of the ocean. The black sky was filled with twinkling stars. On every side of us, red lights pin-pointed the numerous ships in the convoy. I sat there listening to the splash of the wake, and my thoughts were thousands of miles away."

JULY 5, 1957
"In the middle of the ship, below the waterline, there is a vault where all of the 'Top Secret' information is stored. Today, I updated files, rearranged the shelves—and the playboy picture of Marilyn Monroe! At 1300, quarters for a 'man overboard' drill were sounded. Men and officers scurried like ants as they streamed through passageways and ascended ladders. I used a less-frequented ladder toward the bow, greeting the sunshine and fresh air at the starboard gun mounts. On the flight deck, men were running around like water bugs on a pond. Then, each division took shape and, very quickly, 2,500 men were in formation. Each roll and pitch could be felt, as the Randolph cut through the oncoming waves. Looking eastward toward the wave-swept horizon, I suddenly realized that my thoughts were toward the west, which we were quickly leaving behind. At 1430, the order was given to clear all catwalks for a firing drill. Vibrations shook the ship as the guns barked out their intermittent blasts.

"After dinner, I went to the hangar bay where the ship's band was playing. The band was lined up next to the elevator opening, which offered a large rectangular view of the ocean. The rum-tum-tum of the drums and the sharp overtones of the brass echoed through the hangar bay. The audience of dungareed sailors and khakied marines crowded around the band. Three of the songs were, *If you love Suzy like I love Suzy*, *Roll out the Barrel*, and *God Bless America*. The smoothness of the music seems to move right along with the passing waves, as the ship cuts through the miles of sea. After that, I went to the library and read magazines. One of the men was playing soft music on the piano, which offered a relaxing atmosphere. For the last two hours, I have been catching up with these notes, for I had gotten behind when I was working the last few evenings. I'll now take a shower, wait for the evening prayer, and the close of another day. Twice a day we set our clocks ahead an hour. I feel like I'm getting older than I should be every time we do it!"

JULY 6, 1957
"Most of the morning was spent cleaning the compartment and carrying the laundry to the laundry department. We had another man-overboard drill at one o'clock. This time a flare was dropped. The ship cut her engines, slid through the water for several hundred feet, and sat bobbing like a teeter-totter. A boat was lowered, the flare was recovered, and quarters were dismissed. The rest of the afternoon, Thomas, Sam, and I finished assembling the aluminum shelves in the vault. Thomas and Sam worked on the small shelves, while I worked on the remaining large ones. We had four tools: a hammer, chisel, screwdriver, and a pair of pliers. The vault is an L-shaped compartment aft of the bow and on the port side of the ship. A large, steel door is the only opening to it. On the inside of the door, there is a life-sized picture of Jane Mansfield clothed in a very neat, red outfit. The other bulkheads also are covered with pictures of different beauties. A ladder runs directly over the center of the vault, thus forcing you to bend over when passing to the larger shelves.

"As I opened the door, I caught a glimpse of Sam's flying hammer, resounding in loud crashes with each strike. Both Thomas and Sam were laughing and cussing with each boom. Due to the lack of tools, we had to adopt a productive process. While I reassembled each shelf, with the help of the hammer, Sam and Thomas used the screwdriver and pliers to secure the shelves to the column of aluminum siding. We never came out evenly after each phase of work, So we would pressure each other until the phase was completed. This type of pressuring helped to hasten the work, rather than delay it. The two officers bunking adjacent to the vault thought the place was falling apart. The noise had a shattering effect, which sounded like an automotive-pressing department in full swing. At 1500, the job was finished. We all were covered in perspiration and dust. I had been crawling on the floor and looked like a coal miner. We checked the tools in at the tool shop and we got into the shower line.

"That night, we learned that one of the ship's evaporators had broken, thus putting us in condition 'Damp.' Showers are now open only from 4 to 6 a.m. daily. Under these conditions, the ship's complement cannot possibly all have a daily shower.

"I had the 'watch' in the office, where I slept very snugly on two mattresses that I placed on top of the briefing table—commonly known as 'the slab.' Sleeping beside and below the table was Jacabucci. He had what was considered as the most comfortable bed in the office. A large office chair faced the two sides of the room, and eight of briefing chairs were placed parallel to the sides of the room and adjacent to each other. This formed a 'cradle-like' enclosure upon which a mattress rested. The evening prayer was given, and we soon were fast asleep."

July 8, 1957
"Today the weather has taken a turn. Large columns of light-gray clouds blanket the entire sky, stealing the brilliant blue of the water and leaving it a somber dark-gray. The temperature has dropped to 58 degrees. Down below, huge fans push excess heat from the boilers through pathways of ducts, thus heating the ship. At noon, the scene changes, as we push into sunny blue skies.

"We are about 1,100 miles from Gibraltar, cruising steadily along our eastward course. The massive bow of the ship plows through the sea, hurling sheets of foaming waves away from the sides. From the southeast, the island of Flores is visible. Flores is part of the Azores. From 15 miles out, it has a dark, cloudlike appearance, its 3,500-foot, volcanic mountains reaching high into the sky. A fringe of white clouds borders the horizon, while the ocean again changes color to a deep royal-blue. The sun intensifies the white, swirling foam, as the ship continues her plowing. On the horizon, the island takes the shape of an angel-food cake, slightly sloping on its sides.

"The Azores are a group of Spanish islands. Long, flowing wheat fields and farms spread through their valleys, while grape vineyards cling to the mountainsides. A closer look at the islands reveal the rocky cliffs, joined by the green of the trees that grow among the mountains.

"Close to 1600 hours, it was time to take a shower. Thomas and I went down to the head early and found a line of 20 towel-clad men. At 1600, the line began to move. At the entrance to the shower stalls, the yells of the men could be heard as the cold water sprayed down on them. I stepped into a stall, took a deep breath, and sprayed myself with the chilling water. Due to the water shortage, we must first wet down, close the faucet, soap down, and rinse. Back at the compartment, pleasant music flowed in, as we entered a low-frequency band.

"The evening was spent in both work and recreation. Miere and I recorded overlays in the burn log for two hours. We then went below and bought two cokes. Al put on a couple of records, and suddenly the office came to life. We opened a package of crackers that were hoarded from the mess deck. The combination of coke and crackers tasted very good.

"Suddenly, Thomas, Lamarca, and Jacabucci came charging through the office door, exuberant in their joy of finishing their evening's work. We started spinning some hot music, which touched off a discussion of different dance steps. Then, Lamarca and Jacabucci began rocking, rolling, and spinning among the audience of desks, files, and typewriters. On the other side of the table, Thomas and I began a combination of dance steps from Michigan and Mississippi, with me doing an Indian dance step. As the tempo increased, I stepped backward too fast and landed stern-first on two burn bags. Amid all of this turmoil Miere, sat at a table quietly writing his girlfriend, occasionally looking at us with a quizzical grin. Lamarca seemed to have all the rhythm and smoothness of a professional. Thomas, Jacabucci, and I all tried some of his shoulder-to-shoulder turns, shuffling along with each beat of the music.

"After an hour and a half, Thomas and I both bowed out, while Lamarca and Jacabucci continued on until about 0100. We finally rolled the mattresses onto the tables and desks and went to sleep. Early in the morning, I awoke to the steady one-two stomp, one-two stomp of prisoners from the ship's brig, as they passed through the passageway. The small, orange light from the intercom cast a faint beam across the office. I decided to visit the head, so after putting on my shoes, I stepped into the dim passageway and walked around a couple of corners. Suddenly, the stomping began again, and five head-shaven prisoners appeared in the head. Two Marines stood at each end of the file, their wooden clubs ready for action. The prisoners' faces showed neither smirks nor any suggestion of smiles. Their eyes stared straight ahead, creating an expression of complete nothingness. A command was given, and the five robots filed out the door. Their stomps steadily died out as the descended into the dark.

"The Sunday holiday routine is in process. That means that there is no set time to get up, and that you can sleep as long as you like. But there are a few exceptions to this rule, and they affect the men who have the duty on that day. They need to stay at their working stations and carry out only what is required and no more.

"After washing, I stepped down into the semi-darkness of the berthing compartment, where the two night lamps illuminated the room in a dim red, just enough to discern the shapes of bunks, lockers, and pathways. I stepped around a corner, found Thomas, and woke him. After he dressed and washed, we went up the ladder, around to the other side of the ship, and down again to the mess deck. Luckily, at this hour of the morning there were no lines. Steam poured up from beneath the aluminum containers in the mess line, each one holding a different kind of food. We each took a portion of ham and eggs, two cartons of milk, a slice of cantaloupe, and (my favorite) a sweet roll, with apples and white frosting on top. We both left the sweet rolls until last, topping them off with two cups of coffee. We deposited our dirty dishes and hurried up through the maze of planes toward hangar-bay one. As bells rang and the heavy doors rumbled out from the sides toward the center of the ship, we were running to get to the church service. The doors were almost shut when we got there, so we quickly detoured around on a catwalk and entered through one of the folding side panels.

"The chaplain was just stepping up to the altar. High up on the starboard bulkhead, the walnut-brown organ piped out its greeting chords. Blue, white, and khaki uniforms intermingled through the congregation. From the front row, the distinct, semi-bald head of the captain was visible. The Prelude and Call to Worship having ended, the Hymn of Praise and Petition, the Lord's Prayer, and the Choral Response followed. Next, we sang the Hymn of Consecration. Which was followed by the Meditation.

"We then had the Sacrament of the Lord's Supper, which was very impressive. White candles were placed on the rear of the altar, casting fiery beams of light across the golden cross. The men filed to the altar and kneeled in prayer. The chaplain grasped the golden chalice, dipped a piece of bread into the red wine, and administered the sacrament to the kneeling men. After the last man had been blessed, the chaplain sat the chalice between the two golden vases, which held red and white carnations. When everyone was again seated, we stood and sang the Navy hymn, each note resonating through the steel-encased hangar bay:

>   *Eternal Father, strong to save,*
>   *Whose arm doth bind the restless wave,*
>   *Who bids the might ocean deep*
>   *Its own appointed limits keep:*
>   *O hear us when we cry to thee,*
>   *For those in peril on the sea.*
>   *Lord, guard and guide the men who fly*
>   *Through the great spaces of the sky,*
>   *Be with them traversing the air*
>   *In darkening storms and sunlight fair:*
>   *O hear us when we lift our prayer*
>   *For those in peril in the air.*

"The Benediction was given, the Postlude began, and the doors rumbled open, shining the full daylight on the silvery planes. The afternoon was spent sorting five, 80-pound bags of laundry.

"This evening, I went up to the flight deck to catch the sunset. As I stepped through the hatchway, I suddenly was met by a strong wind. Dark clouds loomed overhead, and the sea was running high. The planes were held snugly in place by steel cables, while the strong winds howled through their wings. I braced myself just behind the planes and watched the blinking lights of the destroyer running a quarter-mile behind our wake. I decided to go down on the fantail, where the enclosure would offer protection from the wind. There were about 30 men there. Some were standing and talking, while others sat writing letters.

"The sun was about 20 degrees off the horizon and a cast a beam of whitish-gold light through the hazy sky. A half-mile to the west, a tanker passed in the opposite direction. Her dark hull sat low in the water and ran along with the wind. After five minutes, she was well behind us. Then, the sky put on a very unusual performance. There were three layers of clouds, all crossing in different directions and at different heights. Directly above the ship, the sky was blue, and a layer of white clouds spread out. Toward the horizon, an orchard-like scattering of peach-colored clouds could be seen. Between the white and peach, there was a rib-like formation of light-gray clouds, and on the surface, the dark clouds passed directly over the ship. As the sun dipped lower, the white clouds joined the orchard-shaped ones to create a still more brilliant peach. As the sun dipped lower yet, the orchard finally surrendered to the dark-black color. I stood there for half an hour thinking about many things. After the sun had set, I went below to the library, where I read a couple of magazines."

July 15, 1957

"We have landed in Gibraltar. We were given liberty and ferried to shore. There wasn't much to see except monkeys everywhere! I did manage to buy some shoes and a cashmere sweater, which all were duty-free. Several of the men ordered new duty-free cars, which were to be delivered back west, after our tour. We are leaving Gibraltar and, the sharp sound of the bugle could be heard as quarters for leaving port were sounded. On the flight deck, the band played an array of tunes, while the sun glinted off of their gold-plated instruments. The mountains across the bay rose up in dark shadows behind the hazy sky. A large blanket of puffy clouds hung just above their peaks. The flags on the halyards were whipping in the wind, while large puffs of clouds passed just above the ship. A rumble and clashing of iron could be heard from the façade, as the captain slowly wound the heavy anchor chains out of the clean, green water. The anchor slowly ascended from the water and was secured by the hawser. A cloud of white steam rolled from the whistle, as the ship gave a long, loud blast of departure.

"To our rear, two destroyers drifted behind with the tide. The wind blew streams of smoke from their stacks. Small caps of white waves formed across the bay. A school of porpoises raced through the water, close to our stern. These friendly little guys rolled along together in perfect harmony, pushing up pockets of foam with each dive. Soon, additional groups joined in the fun, making graceful black shadows streaking beneath the green water. Each pair would rise together, exposing their white stomachs at every turn. We couldn't have asked for a more friendly farewell! The ship made a turn to starboard and moved out toward the middle of the straits. The white-rock face of Gibraltar looked more majestic than ever from this distance. You could understand why the Greeks called it the 'Pillar of Hercules.' Clouds formed at the top of the rock, floating there in masses of white. Soon the mountains and the ocean faded away, but the rock stood firm, like a monster in the middle of the sea. The wind increased now that we were away from the shelter of the rock, in the center of the straits. An hour later, we were once again out of sight of land."

Standing, from left, me, Kelly Lyon, and Shelly Schwab. Seated, Diego Abrego.

JULY 30, 1957

"This evening, five of us from the office all went to the ship's variety show. A group from Germany furnished the entertainment. The show was composed of two dancing girls, a boy/girl juggling exhibition, and a male singer. The first number was by the blonde dancer. She had long, silky hair that reached below her shoulders. The light-blonde hair contrasted beautifully with her tanned body!"

August 11, 1957

"We have arrived at the island of Mallorca, which is one of the most beautiful islands in the world. The mountains sit low, providing a feeling of peace and restfulness. The capital city of Palma lies on a flat surface at the base of the mountains. Its tall church steeples and towering walls reflect the pride of this thriving city. A rocky seawall stretches out from the southwestern part of the city. The other half of the bay is protected by a natural, jaw-like portion of land. This is the older section of the city. A cathedral stands on the point of this barrier of land and aggressively attracts your attention toward itself. The distinctive feature of the cathedral is its spires. Our carrier is now anchored out in the bay, away from the city, which necessitates riding launches to the docks. Once in the launch, you get a lively picture of the activity in the bay. On one side, you see a three-masted cargo schooner. Many other schooners are lined up along the wharves, busily loading and unloading cargo. Small sailboats gently glide over the waves. And a long sightseeing boat passes on our left side.

"On land, three small windmills stand along a street that sits only slightly higher than the harbor. Above the main boulevard, you see the fashionable hotels that rise up gently in front of the green mountains. The Hotel Aquaria is the largest in the city, and it ascends in terrace-like fashion, each level offering a patio of spruce and palm trees. Adjacent to Aquaria is the Hotel Victoria, which features a beautiful, blue swimming pool. The pool sits in a white block, bordering the boulevard, while the rectangular main section of the hotel rises up behind it. Each room has a small, semi-circular balcony enclosed with wrought-iron rails.

"Our launch passed the yacht club, where sailing boats of all types were moored. A two-masted sloop rests against the pier. Its hull and cabin are painted black. We learned that this ship belongs to Errol Flynn, who, incidentally, put in a complaint, stating that our liberty launches were creating waves that were detrimental to his boat.

"When we reached the boat landing, we found a stone stairway leading to the top of the wharf. We rounded a corner and soon were right in the midst of the loading and unloading of the cargo schooners. Trucks and horse-drawn wagons line the wharves, while dark-skinned Spanish men unload the cargo. These cargo consists largely of wicker chairs, straw-encased wine jugs, barrels made from freshly cut wood, straw, plumbing fixtures, and wooden boxes. We followed a wrought-iron enclosure for a block to the main boulevard, which is one of the most picturesque in the world. On the corner sat five horse-drawn rigs, each painted a different color. The boulevard is about 100 feet wide and is bordered on each side by flat, gray-stone sidewalks. It has two lanes, for right- and left-hand traffic. In the center is an island, split by a trolley track, and both the island and the sidewalks are lined with tall, green palm trees. The traffic is composed of many different types of autos. One is a foot-high, soapbox-like looking affair that holds two people. The majority of autos resemble our early '30s models. They are square-like, with running boards, curved fenders, and domed headlights. Occasionally, you can spot an American-built auto but not very often.

"The rest of the traffic is composed of many motorcycles and bicycles. And red trolley cars run through the middle of the island, each one crowded with people. Their undercarriages comprise four iron wheels. The car body extends out on each side, giving the trolley a rocky motion as it clicks along. As we advance farther along the boulevard, the beauty increases. Small gardens of colorful flowers and sparkling-green grass spread out from the sidewalks and along the islands. A few blocks farther, you see a more modern style of architecture, which extends for three blocks. You can get the most for your money when you rent a rig for a few pesos. This way, you have time to see all of the little things, like the different tourists, their types of clothing, hair styles, and nationalities.

"Once in a while, you catch the aroma of the horses. The streets are kept spotlessly clean and neat. All along the sidewalks, we see a heterogeneous assemblage of tourists, while only here and there do we spot a native islander. If you prefer a swim, you stop at the Victoria Hotel. For 20 pesos, we can change our clothes and use all the facilities at the hotel. The small dressing rooms are called cottages. You step into one, open a hatch, get a bag from a girl, close the hatch, change into your bathing suit, open the hatch, give the girl your clothing, and follow the winding stairway up to the pool.

"The pool is L-shaped, with the diving board at the end of the shorter leg. Stones laid in red rock form the foundation for the board. Flowers of many colors grow near the near the pool. A six-foot-wide tile walkway boarders the pool. At the end of the longer leg there is a separate round-shaped pool for the children. Also at the end is a gentle slope of steps that lead right into the pool. On the side, facing the boulevard, are chairs and awnings for those who wish to stay out of the sun. A garden with plants and brilliant-red flowers divides the pool and the patio. Two steps down from the pool, you are on the patio or outside the restaurant. Two spruce trees angle out of the marble-laid floor. Adjacent to them is a palm tree.

"For 15 pesetas, the waiter will bring you a very good and very strong drink. Each drink is about a third liquor! Three or four of these really will get your head spinning. The view was very nice, as a tanned European beauty held her knife and fork in her right and left hands, respectively, laying either down only to drink. The method of holding silverware here is much different than the way Americans do it. Their method expedites the eating process, which a necessity, due to the many courses served. For 15 pesetas, you can buy a chicken, beef, or ham sandwich, served with lettuce, tomatoes, mayonnaise, and anchovy-stuffed olives. The straws are made from some type of reed or straw and have a pleasant taste. A Tom Collins tastes very good through them!

"The shadows lengthen as the sun creeps closer and closer toward the mountains. You order a couple of drinks and watch the bathers as they splash across the pool. The orchestra forms under the wooden trellis and begins playing romantic music. The sun sets behind the mountains and a fresh breeze moves in from the sea. Soon, dusk encompasses the city, leaving the mountains in a mass of portentious shadows. The whole area is illuminated by its variety of lights. Underwater lights throw their beams out across the floor of the pool. The lights under the fountain penetrate through the spray, giving the water a silvery-white appearance. Small, rectangular lights shine softly out of the rock enclosures that surround the green plants and flowers. Young ladies, dressed in fresh, cool-looking cocktail dresses, stroll by our table, with their high heels clicking on the marble floor. A private party gathers in the dancing area, so we walk down the sandstone steps, through the wide glass doors, and out onto the parking lot adjacent to the boulevard.

"A long, black taxi pulls up to the hotel entrance and leaves a couple of men at the door. We inquire as to the price for driving us to the Olympia Club. Twenty-five pesetas sounds pretty reasonable, so we step in and head down the boulevard. We turn up a street that boarders a beautiful park. The other side of the street is composed mostly of sidewalk cafes. After a succession of many streets and boulevards, we pull up to what looks like a large gymnasium. After paying for the taxi and walking inside, we find that the outer appearance of the building was quite deceptive—beginning with the fact that it was completely void of a roof. The middle of the square on the ground level is the dance floor, made of gray, diamond-shaped tiles. Five levels of terraced stone lead down to the dance floor on three sides of the square. An assortment of small tables, chairs, and railings are included on each level. Each table is covered by a patterned tablecloth and a small, green or yellow lamp. On one side of the square is a small group of men who make up the music combo, dressed in black pants, white shirts, and gray vests.

"Once again we see tourists from many countries. Everyone is well-dressed in light, colorful, Summer wear. We walk through a doorway and around to the far side, ascending to the third terrace. The fast beat of the music flows through the square and up into the open sky, where the moon and stars paint a whiteness through the passing clouds. We find a table under a young oak tree, which is at the end of the line of six trees that grow along the wall. A large, white trellis spreads out just below the leaves that move with the wind. We order our drinks and, when we get the bill, we're very surprised at the price—50 pesetas each—or about a dollar in American money. After finishing our drinks, we order another round, this time nursing them along. After nursing three more rounds, we begin a conversation with five French girls, who are sitting next to our table. The conversation goes on with much talking and very little understanding, given the language barrier. We finally find out they are from Toulouse, which is 600 miles from Paris. They all are in their early 20s and single. Their occupations are secretarial and they will be in Palma for two weeks. Two of the girls are blondes and the other three are brunettes. After talking for 20 minutes, we ask the girls to dance. We accomplished absolutely nothing in our conservations with them and just concentrated on dancing. I asked my partner her name and she said it was Claudia. She has blue eyes and dark eyebrows. She is wearing a blue cocktail dress, speckled with white polka dots. You naturally indicate to her that she has a very pretty dress. With a soft smile, she replies that she made it herself. That concludes the conversation and we go on dancing to all the songs that are played. When I returned to the table with this young lady, we found an interpreter, which helped out a lot.

"Suddenly, the orchestra struck up an introduction for the dancers in the forthcoming floor show. The violin, accordion, and saxophone begin a fast song, and the lights are turned upon a young senorita, who comes spinning out onto the dance floor. She is wearing a beautifully colored lace shirt and white blouse. Red flowers adorn her black hair. She spins and weaves her arms over her head, clicking her castanets with every beat of the music. The expressions on her face and the emphasis in her singing flow in harmony with the music. Her skirt whirls in a complete circle, folding like a fan with each turn and unfurling again as she spins in the opposite direction. She twirls, turns, and spins with such speed that the flowers fly onto the tile floor. In spite of the speed of the dance, it's done with the utmost in precision and grace. She takes one last spin, falls to the floor, and the dance ends. Two more senoritas appear, the last one in a beautiful, white dress. The show ends with a trio of two senoritas and a senor. The dancing and the music goes on with increasing gusto, but we must leave this place in order to get back to the ship in time. We bid farewell to the French girls, leaving them with an invitation to visit our ship the following day."

OCTOBER 3, 1957
"Today was a perfect day to go ashore in Rhodes, Greece. A refreshing Fall breeze blew in across the choppy, blue bay, while the mountains of Turkey spread out in a long line on the horizon, an occasional streak of clouds cutting behind their peaks. At 0900, the liberty launch crosses the choppy bay and enters the harbor, sending swells of waves up against the rocks and pilings. On one side of the harbor, a small, fortress-like structure stood. It was made entirely of light-brown rocks that were chipped into squares many years ago. A white lighthouse stood above the roof of the structure, marking the harbor entrance at night. A small stretch of rocks connected this structure with the boulevard bordering the harbor. The boat landing, as well as the piers that enclosed the harbor, were made of light-gray stones that appeared almost white from the reflection of the sun. Everything looked clean and neat along the boulevard. A stretch of sidewalk bordered a small park of green-spruce and palm trees. In the middle of the boulevard stood a circular fountain, and the inner portion was made in the form of a water lily. To the left of the park was a red-brick boulevard. Twenty feet from the building was a brick tower that reached as high as the pointed roof of the building. At the top of the tower, there was an enclosed bell. On the other side of the building, there was a whole string of shops and sidewalk cafes.

"The streets all pointed upward from the boulevard, so Thomas, Andy, and I chose one leading to a bicycle shop. We each selected a bike and gave the man a dollar for six hours. We mounted them and began pedaling through the streets. We went uphill for a couple of blocks, then turned left and sped downhill toward the center of the town. The wind whistled past our ears as we sped down the long hill. The gardens were very large, exhibiting green trees and multi-colored flowers. We turned right at the bottom of the hill and rode up to the wall of the Old City. The crudely cut blocks rose 40 feet into the air, obscuring everything except the sky and clouds. We peddled our bikes along the wide boulevard that paralleled the wall. After peddling for three blocks, we passed under a large archway that led through the wall and into the Old City. Inside the walls, the streets narrowed, their surface being made from small, rounded stones that gave you a bumpy ride as the bicycle went over them. We passed small, eight-foot-wide shops and tall, narrow houses packed tightly together. Children played barefooted in the streets, and here and there you would see a cat sleeping in the sun. The sun shined brightly down on the light-tan roofs of the narrow houses and left its warmth on everything it touched.

"We rode laterally through the town and entered another archway that cut through the wall and entered a bridge that crossed a wide ravine. The bridge was 10 feet wide and made entirely of stone. At the bottom of the ravine, numerous brown goats grazed on grass and bushes that grew near a small creek. We stopped on the bridge and took a few shots of them with Thomas' camera. On the other side of the bridge, we entered a small parkway and turned down a path that led under spruce trees. Red flowers grew from the low bushes that bordered the rocky path. We turned right and bumped along another path that ran next to a rock wall. The wall was two feet high, and it separated the parkway from the slopes of the ravine. The goats at the bottom of the ravine looked like deer, as they moved in and out of the thick bushes. We parked our bikes and caught a few more pictures of them.

"About 10 kids came running up to our bicycles and began asking for candy and cigarettes. When they saw us taking pictures of the goats, they began throwing stones at them. We started off, and the kids came running after us. We finally lost them when we reached the corner. Here, we found another boulevard that curved around the outer edge of the parkway and then climbed straight up a long hill. As we moved up the boulevard, we encountered lines of spruce trees growing out of the stone sidewalks. Their trunks rose up and their branches formed a long, green archway over the street. We now were in a much nicer residential section. The homes sat behind low, brick walls and had painted-stucco exteriors, with tiled roofs. Each house was surrounded by gardens of flowers and bushes.

"We met a couple of boys, who much to our surprise, were Americans. We asked if there were any places to buy any cold drinks. They replied that there weren't but that we could have some water if we went to their house. We followed them for half a block and stopped in front of their house. The boys went into the house and came back out with their mother, who was carrying a tray of glasses and a pitcher of water. She was a young woman in her middle or late 20s. We asked about her family, where the children went to school, how they liked living there, etc. She was very nice and gave us some tips on things to see and do. We finished our water and thanked them. It really seemed good to talk to American people again.

"The road kept winding upward, past several excavated ruins. We stopped at one point where the road turned and shot some pictures of the ship in the bay and the city below us. We were standing on the edge of a bluff that was about 1,000 feet high. We could see the rocky shoreline below us, easily distinguishing the features under the water. We started off again, finally reaching the top of the bluff, where the road leveled and clung to the fringe of the high cliffs. The topography up there was mostly clay and rocks, with occasional clumps of grass growing under a scattering of trees. A few rust-colored marble pillars rose up from the red clay and rocks, leaving the sky, city, and mountains behind them. This was all that remained of the once-proud temple of two millennia past. We parked our bicycles on the side of the road and snapped a couple of shots of the old ruins. We walked up a small rise and sat on a bench that faced the sea. This location afforded another beautiful view. The ocean stretched far out to the Turkish mainland. Along the shoreline, the dark rocks changed to white, as the waves cascaded over them. The beach stretched far down the length of the island, vanishing in a promontory of dark mountains.

"While we were sitting observing the view, a brown bird came out of the cliffs, drifted along with the wind, and when he got directly in front of us, he stopped and stayed in one place, with his wings displayed for just a few movements. He seemed as though he was being polite to us and letting us get a good picture, or maybe he was just observing us. It was very good in any respect, because it made for an unusual picture. We once again mounted and passed the old temple that sat a little off the road. The road made a U-turn, moved up over a hill, and then wound down for a mile and a half past ruins, excavations, homes, spruce trees, and finally past the shops and houses on the outskirts of the city. We made one last, long turn around a curve and came out on the road that lay just above the ocean. We pulled up in front of a bar, parked our bicycles, and walked in. The name of the place was 'The American Bar' (there's one in every port!). We ordered three beers that cost us 30 cents apiece. The beer was a Dutch brand and tasted good after exercising so hard. And we took our time drinking.

With Diego Abrego on our day off.

"Once more on our way, we headed up the road that followed the ocean. The sun was getting lower in the sky and struck a glistening glare on the face of the ocean. We peddled up a long hill to a point where the city stopped. The road weaved through some huge rocks that protruded out from the bluff and stood up on the other side, facing the sea. We looked up and could see where we had been a little less than an hour earlier. From this point, the road took a long, gradual descent, terminating at a line of small houses on the side of the cliffs. The beach wound through a maze of boulder-shaped rock formations. They ended where the village began and the beach leveled out into a sandy plain. Several colorful, sturdily built, wooden boats hugged the shoreline.

"The road leveled off and peddling became more difficult, as we now were riding into the wind. Looking up along the cliffs, you could see small groups of spruce trees. As we passed the houses, a whole swarm of barefooted children ran out of the house, each one holding a can of beer and shouting "beer, beer." They all were only about six or seven years old. A young, dark-haired girl in her teens sat in the doorway of one of the houses, sewing a dress, while an old man sat looking at us. Motor scooters and motorcycles raced by us, quickly disappearing over the small hill that crossed a bridge at the other side. It was surprising that most of the men riding the scooters were older. They all were dressed in sports coats, slacks, and hats. Apparently, we were on the road that led to the airport, and we decided not to pedal that far, so we turned around and headed back.

"After turning around, the wind was now to our backs and it pushed us along at a good rate of speed. We followed the same course back, winding our way along the beach, entering the residential section, passing by the sidewalk cafes, and on toward the old walls again. A young, blonde gal entered the boulevard in front of us, her long hair blowing with wind. She was pedaling in our direction, so we just stayed behind her. She finally turned into the Old City, where we had entered earlier that afternoon. I continued going straight, while Thomas kept his eyes glued on the girl. He was moving a faster than me and collided with my bicycle. I went down, breaking the fall with my hands. Thomas got a good bruise on his shin but was able to keep his stability. I got up unhurt, and we were once more on our way. This time, we entered the walled city and came out on the other side, still outside of the main wall. A large boulevard led itself around the bay and bordered the wall. This place gave the wall an appearance of great height and length. By now, the sun was behind the other side of the wall, thus leaving the boulevard and our side of the wall in huge shadows. The boulevard was split by a garden. We rode along the wall and finally entered at its extremity. We caught glimpses of churches, gardens, and windmills, taking pictures of these and several others of small children and girls. We returned our bicycles, had supper at an outdoor café, and caught the 2000 launch back to the ship, thus ending a beautiful day of liberty in Rhodes, Greece. Our next port of call returned us back to Palma de Mallorca.

"As Christmas approached, the ship had an open house, and hundreds of people from Palma de Mallorca came aboard. The ship's band held a concert and played for dancing in the hangar bay. Diego Abrego, one of my best friends, met a pretty Spanish senorita named Antonia. She invited him to come to her mountain village the next day. So Diego, myself and two other shipmates pooled our money and rented a taxi. The village was 40 miles away. It was a beautiful, sunshiny afternoon. The car moved slowly on the curvy road up through green meadows and into the mountains. In the distance, we noticed the spires of the Catholic church.

"Once in the village, we noticed families taking their customary afternoon strolls up and down the streets. We did not know where Antonia lived, so we asked a man for her address. He gave it to us, and we walked to her house, knocked at the door, and asked for her. The servant said that she was at the movie theater, so we went there. At the theater, a 10-year-old boy was taking tickets. Noticing that we were sailors, he asked, 'Are there any negroes on your ship?' We asked why and he said that he had never seen one and wondered what they looked like. We replied, 'Of course, we have many fine negroes aboard.' In the meantime, Antonia's father had sent her tutor to meet us at a small outside café and had fetched Antonia from the movie theater. Most of their conversation was in Spanish, so just she and Diego carried on talking. While entertaining ourselves, we had glasses of champagne and some snacks and said our farewells, as the sun was beginning to set. Diego corresponded with Antonia for several months, but he decided not to make any stronger connections.

"The next day, we boarded a tour bus to take us up to another little village with a monastery called the Royal Carthusian Monastery of Valldemossa. Here we encountered some younger children with a folk dance group from Mallorca. We took many great pictures." [Ironically, 60 years later, I had Diego send a letter to the village to see if they could locate the dancers. The girl in the picture was 12 years old at the time, and she sent a nice reply, saying that it was her in the original picture with her brother, who had since passed away. She still was living on the island of Mallorca, with her husband and two grown children, and still danced with the folk group.]

Young dancers in Valldemossa, Spain.

"Our ship had just anchored outside of the Port of Naples, Italy, when Shelly Schwabski, who we called 'Ski' for short, asked if I wanted to sign up for a tour of Rome. I said, 'Yes, let's do it!' The next day. 25 crew members were aboard the train heading north, passing by flat farmland and left-over traces from World War II. We arrived in Rome and stayed in a small hotel. The next day, we toured the ancient Roman ruins, the Trevi Fountain, and lots of churches and museums. Ski and I rented bicycles and rode 20 miles to the outskirts of the city to learn more about the lifestyles of the people. They were very friendly and took pictures of us. At the end of the day. I was exhausted and took a nap back at our hotel. I awoke later that evening and Ski was gone. Thinking it was earlier, I showered and ventured out through the streets. Finally, I found out that it was midnight and everything was closing. I found a small café that was still open and talked to a friendly signorina, whose sister had married a serviceman. I finally made it back to our hotel room and found Ski fast asleep in bed.

"We were blessed the next day to get a tour of the Vatican and an audience with the Pope, who in 1957 was Pope Pius XII. We were bused there and walked across an enormous courtyard and into the church, whose walls were covered with Michelangelo's paintings. The sun shining through the colored glass produced brilliant reflections of the images. We were then ushered up to the audience chamber and stood in a 30x30-foot enclosure. We watched as military personnel from other countries were seated. Ski and I positioned ourselves at the front of the enclosure for a closeup view when the pope was to pass by. All was quiet as we waited. We assumed that it would be a peaceful and quiet atmosphere. After quite a wait, we were told that the pope was making his way toward the chapel. Our chaplain said, 'When he comes through the doorway, I want you all to yell, Hip, hip, hooray, hip, hip, hooray as loud as you can!'

"Soon, Pope Pius appeared, sitting atop a platform borne by 10 men. The first shouts were from the Spanish sailors. They shouted, 'Viva la pope, viva la pope.' Soon the entire chapel erupted in cheers in a mixture of languages. Ski, who is Jewish, and I, who was baptized as a Lutheran when I was eight years old, both felt we belonged there. Behind us, the Catholics were waving their beads and hitting our heads. As the procession approached us, Ski reached out and touched the pope's hand. I stretched out but just missed touching him. He addressed the crowd in several different languages. He blessed everyone, Catholics and non-Catholics alike. It was a very exciting experience, and I will never forget it."

My parents and brother, Tom, came to see me after my return from Europe.

"It wasn't long after our visit to Italy that we were discharged in New York City. I went home with Ski for several days. His mother worked in a tailor shop, so I picked up a suit and sports coat to get ready for my job search, once I got back to Michigan. My time in the U.S. Navy turned out to be a great adventure, plus it really matured me. I leave the remembrances of my sea life with a poem that I really enjoyed.

SAILING HOME

"What is it the billowing waves impart,
and repeat and repeat with each dash
What is the pounding in my heart?
I'm sailing home at last.
The salt spray stings on the naked cheek
and the wind sings in the mast,
but it only sings because it knows,
I'm sailing home, at last.
Was it centuries since we sailed away
Out of the harbor there,
or was it only yesterday
I don't know, nor care.
For gone are the lonely nights and the days
mid tropical isles alone
and gone is the hunger countenanced there,
At last I'm sailing home.
And tho the sailor sails the seas
and in distance places roam
There is no "call" that's quite so sweet
as the call, "I'm Sailing Home."

With Fred Kalhorn in Sun Valley, ID.

Chapter 8

Building Airplanes

IN THE FALL OF 1958, I received an honorable discharge from the Navy. The United States was in a recession, which made it difficult to find employment, so I painted 11 homes in South Haven, having a beautiful Fall to accomplish the jobs. I saved $600, enough to fly to Seattle, where the Boeing Airplane Company was busy building B52 bombers and Bomarc Antiaircraft missiles. My parents drove me to Bangor, MI, to catch the train to Chicago. I had money from the Navy, plus the $600 painting money, a suit, a sports coat and a few other clothes. This was my total net worth.

Later that evening, I flew on a four-engine Lockheed airliner to Seattle. The engine propellers revved up to a roar, and I was off to the Pacific Northwest. Early the next morning, after a six-hour flight, I looked out the window at the Boeing Field Airport. The plane touched down, and I disembarked and got a room at the Roosevelt Hotel in Seattle. The next day, I went to the Boeing employment office and filled out an application. I stayed at the Seattle Elks Club until I could get my bearings and get settled in somewhere. The first Sunday, I decided to go to the Congregational Church, where, believe it or not, I prayed that I would land a position with the Boeing Company. My prayers came true the following week. I was interviewed and offered a job in the personnel department of Boeing's Bomarc Missile Division as a personnel representative, responsible for factory operations.

I was excited and took a bus from the 4th Street Elks Club to the old Ford Plant, site of the Bomarc production. My supervisor, Fred Holtman, didn't have much time to train me that first day because he had to fly back East to do some recruiting. He drove me to the Developmental Center and showed me how to use the time clock, then gave me a stack of procedure manuals and told me to read them over. After eight hours of reviewing hundreds of procedures, I was anxious to clock out at the time-keeping station. I got there just before the end of the first shift. I heard a loud buzzer go off, and—out of nowhere—a thundering herd of people came running for the time clock. I barely was able to punch out. I managed to find the bus stop for the route back to the Elks Club. Needless to say, those beers at the bar tasted good. I was lucky to be an Elks Club member. I made lots of good acquaintances and learned about the Seattle area.

A couple of days later my boss returned. He was very busy and needed to get about 100 employees' folders to the corporate office. He introduced me to Bill Hartstein, the manpower coordinator for the division, who was a cheerful person. Bill told me, "Take these two boxes over to the corporate office and give them to Jack Healey. I took the Boeing bus to corporate headquarters and met Mr. Healey. We immediately went through the 100 folders in surprisingly fast time. I then took the Boeing bus back and left the folders in Bill Hartstein's office. That was my first overtime pay!

Soon after beginning my job at Boeing, I was fortunate to find a room that rented for $25 a month. It was located on Capitol Hill in Seattle, not that far from the plant. Fortunately another roommate, Rick Palazzo, who also worked at Boeing, had a car, so I rode with him to work every day. In the mornings on our way to work, we ate breakfast for 35 cents at another boarding house in the same neighborhood and most of the time stopped for dinner on the way home for 75 cents. The food was excellent, especially the homemade pies for dessert. Rick, who was engaged to be married, invited me on many Sundays to his future in-laws for great dinners. It wasn't until the next Spring, when I was 25 years old, that I bought my first car—a 1953

Ford and the first of the five '53 Fords that I owned over the years. They were very dependable and easy to work on.

First rental house on Capitol Hill in Seattle—top-left dormer room for $25 a month.

The first Winter in Seattle I joined the Boeing Ski club. Later on, I became acquainted with Charles Kelly, who worked at the corporate office. He was a gregarious guy and arranged lots of TGIF parties. He picked up the nickname, "Charley Brown," from the Charles Shultz comic strip. In the Spring, the ski club drove cars to Sun Valley for a fun week. My good friend, Fred Kalhorn, was visiting me from Michigan, so he came along. On Friday nights, the club rented the third floor of the Washington Athletic Club in Seattle. I met several new female friends, some whom I dated.

In 1960, I moved and shared a small cottage on Mercer Island with Ervin Vernon. We worked together at Boeing. I met a new circle of his friends, most of them were on the Stevens Pass ski patrol. Every weekend, we would ski all day and party Saturday night at Skykomish. It was the early '60s and we danced to the "twist." Summers were spent on Puget Sound on Erv's 26-foot Blanchard knockabout sailboat.

Soon, I met a string of young girls and guys who attended the social group. We had picnics, cruises, beach parties, and dances. I recall at one of the house parties seeing an attractive girl far across the living room. Hoping to talk to her, I joggled my way through about 30 people, only to find she had vanished. The house was crowded almost body to body.

Ervin Vernon, my Mercer Island roommate.

The Bomarc Missile Production Division was a small division in a large corporation, employing roughly 5,000 employees. The missile was designed to intercept and shoot down Russian bombers during the Cold War. Things could be coordinated easily and effectively, and most things got done by talking one on one. We had a small personnel department, and everyone was friendly and happy with their bosses and counterparts. I was responsible for servicing the Manufacturing Department. I wanted to know what every section did and asked the supervisors lots of questions.

The supervisor in final assembly invited me to go fishing in Puget Sound in a nice boat that he had built himself. I hooked something that took the whole spool of line from the reel, probably a seal or a huge salmon, but lost it.

Eventually, I was assigned to the second shift, an assignment that seemed to go to single people. I did a bit of career-development work with younger people, and lots of employees requested transfer applications, where I would advise employees when job openings were available inside the Boing Company.

One day in June, my first Summer of work, I was told that tours of the factory were being planned. They were to be conducted weekly, beginning at 7 p.m. Guess who was to give the "History of the Boeing Company" speech and lead the group through the plant? You guessed it! Me! I was given a four-page copy of the speech and had two weeks to learn it. I practiced it with friends who I knew from swimming at Madison Park Beach during the day. Finally, during the first tour, I mistakenly said the current president (what now would be CEO) was Bill Boeing, instead of Bill Allen, and did a little bit of stuttering during the remainder of it.

My first car—a 1953 Ford.

But the following week's tour included members from the Corporate Offices and my boss's boss. I was very nervous when the microphone was put around my neck. I breathed hard into the speaker to make sure it was working, but there was no volume amplitude! I was standing there in front of this crowd of important people and, in my mind, I thought. "Oh damn!" But, to my surprise, every word of my four-page speech flowed smoothly until the last sentence, where I had a slight pause. Of course, the corporate PR person needed something to report about the speech and said it was not smooth. However, my boss' boss told the personnel director that I did an excellent job! My one-man tour was a far cry from today's tours at the Everett (WA) plant, where hundreds of people are involved in showing thousands of tourists through the plant each year.

Unfortunately, funding for the Bomarc program was cut and the division had a gradual reduction, and most of the employees were integrated into the Military Aircraft Division at Plant Two. Since I was working second shift, I still had responsibility for the phasing-out work at the Bomarc factory location.

Because the Military Division was overstaffed, it had more personnel work for us to accomplish. We subsequently were trained to investigate employee suggestions for creating savings for the company. We looked at the existing processes and compared them with the proposed methods, subtracting the savings from one to the other and sending them on for payment. This experience was helpful later on when I worked in the Industrial Engineering Department. In 1961, I was transferred to the Personnel Department of the Commercial Airplane Division in Renton. There, a Work Simplification program was initiated throughout the division. The study that I originated was titled "Reduce Employee Transit Time To-and-From the Factory." I suggested sending personnel representatives to the factory, which eliminated employees' excessive time away from their work, therefore saving the company money and speeding up production. It was a good concept, but it didn't sit too well with the personnel director, since it would cut back his empire.

My personnel supervisor previously had worked in the Industrial Engineering Division and arranged a transfer for me as a methods analyst in the 707 Final Assembly Section, where I learned the basics of operating plan management and development. I designed large bar charts of the jobs that were on order. Every day, we would evaluate the status, coloring out jobs that had been completed. After six, months, I was reassigned to Minor Assembly. I was trained to use time-standards books and how to apply time study to specific jobs. I was given special assignments to justify new tools and alternate processes. All of the methods analysts were asked to submit their ideas on how to save the company money.

Blueprints were sent to small buildings all over the factory, taking up valuable production space. I proposed a pneumatic-piping system to transport them from the central blueprint room when and where they were needed. My idea saved Boeing millions of dollars. Eventually, I was assigned to a special section and given the title of instrumentation and refurbishment coordinator for the first three 727 airliners. Our responsibilities included installation of flight-testing equipment in final assembly and making an operating plan for removals after flight testing and restoring the airplanes for delivery to Pan American Airlines. It was fun meeting for breakfasts with the airline representatives and the production-team supervisors. The program was completed thousands of dollars under budget and six weeks ahead of schedule. The manufacturing manager made sure that I got a promotion for my hard work.

In 1987, I returned to Boeing to work on the 747-500 airliner. Innovations in technology were taking place in operating a jet airliner. The flaps, rudders, ailerons, etc. had been hard-wired to the cockpit. The new system eliminated most of the wiring to and from the cockpit. The 747-500 was the first airplane design not to use a mock-up of the duct work and wiring; the company decided that the new computer-aided design system would work in its place.

Unfortunately, because production rates had to be maintained, the tests in final assembly were made later on at Paine Field, rather than on the production line. There were so many malfunctions that 14 airliners had to be stripped down and corrections made on all of them. And the corrections were made at the same time that flight testing was in its final stages. Industrial Engineering assigned a special unit of 20 people to Paine Field to coordinate the changes. Finally, after a year, all 14 planes were finished and the production lines gradually got back on schedule. After this happened, six of us were sent to the time-study section. We were trained in the standard system that the military uses and other less-detailed civilian methods. I can say that I've time-studied every manufacturing classification and climbed inside of wings, fuel tanks, and in every area of airplanes and supporting equipment in the plant.

Later on in 1990, I was reassigned to the Industrial Engineering Section that supported the 767 Tooling Engineering Design and Fabrication Shop. I was surprised to find out that, over time, an airplane's wing components wear out, due to their constant flexing in flight. When a sub-assembly of parts showed excessive wear, a Tool-Design Request (TDR) was written. An engineer made up the plans, the tooling drawings, and the paperwork that went to the Industrial Engineering Tooling Support Group. My job was to review the TDRs and determine what the Tool-Fabrication Shop needed to do to make the tools that were used in the Assembly Shops. I had to estimate the amount of time it would take for the change and schedule a meeting with the tool-design engineer, the tooling fabrication supervisor and myself. We would discuss what was needed and how many man hours it would take to get it completed. We also placed it in a priority listing. I was surprised to learn that the TDR backlog was in the thousands, just for the wings. Fortunately, changes that were in proximity in a wing area all were all done at the same time, which speeded up the process.

Today, more than 20 years later, the wings are fabricated almost 100 percent from high-strength, composite materials. The wings are made in a large mold; the material is heated, and out comes the new wing. Thousands of aluminum parts are eliminated, thus saving time and materials and speeding up the production line. Times have changed with technology and computers. Gone is the time when I could talk to somebody "one-on-one" and the results would be on the shop floor the next day. Now, the Industrial Engineering Department at Boeing is incorporated into the Planning Department. The wide scope of duties has shrunk into specialized responsibilities. Every year, we have an "Old Timers Dinner" in Kent, WA, for retirees, where we share many memories. Usually, a keynote speaker from the company will be there to bring us up to date on various programs.

Standing across the street from the Boeing Everett plant, from where I retired.

Joanne Zink and I while on leave from the Navy.

Chapter 9

Social Activities/Dating

WHEN I WAS 12, PAUL SHIELDS' PARENTS built a rumpus room above the garage of their house. World War II was coming to an end, and the jitterbug was the rage of the younger generation. Some of the older junior-high girls would come over to the rumpus room and teach us how to dance. Those sessions kept us busy during the Winter months. During eighth grade, some of the mothers would have parties for the boys and girls. At first, we didn't have formal dates, but later on we paired off, guy and girl. Cathy Cane's mother was quite liberal and allowed us to play "spin the bottle." The couples sat in a circle and the bottle was spun. When it stopped at a couple they kissed! This sometimes led to "puppy love" relationships.

Marjorie Pringle was my first girlfriend. When Spring came, our group would play softball on the beach. When I turned 14, I got a driver's license and double dated in the family car. Sometimes we parked outside of town and turned on the radio. On two occasions, my dad had to come and jumpstart the battery. Marilee Urch became a close friend from the eighth grade to her first semester of college, after which she became a flight attendant and finished college later.

When we entered 10th grade, the girls began dating older guys. Most of my dates were with several girls. I did not want a "steady" date. After football and basketball games, we had dances in the girls' gym. I always asked someone to go to Mike's Drive-in for a hamburger and milkshake. Finally, in the Fall of my junior year I began dating Edna Mae Stream. She was a cheerleader and her mother had been a ballerina. She kept me busy going to too many social activities, so we broke up. That Spring, I invited Virginia Royal, who was my Aunt Lettie's niece, to the Prom. She lived in Dearborn, MI, and the following Summer she stayed in South Haven with my uncle Walter and aunt Lettie, so I dated her all Summer. We spent many evenings on the front porch swing. She attended the University of Michigan, so we corresponded and I went to see her and her parents. They were a wonderful family. When I was senior, I asked Dorothy Vogel, who was a freshman, to the Prom. I noticed her one evening at Arkins News Agency and asked one of her friends if she thought Dorothy Ann would like to go to a movie with me. We dated to the end of July, when she moved to Long Beach, CA.

Virginia Royal.

The following Summer, she came back to South Haven, where we continued to see each other. Soon afterwards, she moved to San Diego with her parents. After graduation from high school, she enrolled in Western Michigan University as a freshman when I was a senior. We both had outside jobs and had little time for each other. We dated for the first semester, but later on I told her to date some other guys, since I had been the only she had ever dated. She still washed my clothes and considered me her favorite. Later, after I entered the Navy, we decided to end our relationship. By then, she was living in Detroit with her aunt.

Dorothy Ann Vogel.

During the Summer of 1954, I dated Margaret Edmonton, who was working as a waitress at Mendelson's Resort and attended Indiana University. When we returned to our college classes, we decided we would remain friends. During my first one-month leave from the Navy, I dated Joanne Zink, after my sister, Adelaide, fixed me up with her. We enjoyed my parents' brand new Plymouth Fury convertible. She was athletic and we swam, played golf, and partied for 30 days.

She went with my parents to the airport to see me off. Afterward, she dated my cousin, Wayne Fritz, who was starting his 30-day Navy leave. I always called Wayne my "bird-dogging" cousin from that day on. I'll always remember the fun 30 days I spent with Joanne. Before I dated her, she dated Jim Dunn, another Navy guy on his 30-day leave. It wasn't too long after going back on duty that I got a "Dear John" letter from Joanne.

South Haven cheerleaders—Cathy Cain, Pat Brown, and Edna Stream.

Bob Thomas, a close friend, fellow athlete, and one-third Native American, lived next door to Fred Kalhorn. We played basketball in the hay loft of Fred's parents' barn. Bob was the quarterback on our high school football team, a guard on the basketball team, and shortstop on the baseball team. We double dated a lot with his cheerleader girlfriend, Pat Brown, and my girlfriend, Edna Mae Stream when we were juniors in high school. Pat has been a wonderful connection to our high school Class of 1952 to this day. We call her Auntie Pat and she lets us know good news (about reunions, of which there have been many) and sad news, when classmates pass away.

I believe that the experiences that I had with all the fine young ladies mentioned thus far had a great influence on my life. When I arrived in Seattle in 1958, I remember thinking, somewhere here is the person who I'm going to marry. Luckily for me, that someone turned out to be the love of my life!

My friend, Jim Morris.

Skiing in Sun Valley, ID.

Chapter 10

Jack and Jill Went Up the Hill...

I MET JILL JOHNSON AT STEVENS PASS in the Cascade Mountains of Washington. It was a beautiful, sunshiny March day in 1963, when I rode up to Stevens Pass to go skiing with my roommate, Erv Vernon, who was on the ski patrol. I was skiing alone and, at the bottom of the Big Chief double-chair lift, I approached the "singles" waiting line. I spied an attractive blonde and quickly slid in beside her and asked, "Is it OK to ride up with me?" She said, "Sure!" We both scooted into position and the chair caught us and swept us into the air, toward the top of the mountain (Like in the fairy tale—the *real* Jack and Jill went up the hill!). We began talking and found that we'd both been to Europe recently. I introduced myself: "I'm Jack." And she said, "I'm Jill." When we reached the top of the Seventh Heaven lift, I asked, "Do you want to ski down with me?" I looked back, and she was right behind me. We took several more runs, and later I asked if she would like to go swimming with me on Thursday.

Thursday finally came and I drove quickly from the Renton Boeing Plant to my home on Mercer Island, where I lived with Erv. I cleaned up and drove to the Seattle Elks Club. After parking, I patiently waited for Jill, who soon arrived in her white, 1963 VW bug. We proceeded into the dressing rooms and met at the pool, at which time I noticed that she looked very nice in her white bathing suit. I also noticed that she was a good swimmer, as we swam laps for quite a while. Afterward, I asked if she wanted to go and have a beer. We each got in our cars and drove a short distance to a local pub. When it came time to pay, I found that, in my haste, I had forgotten my wallet. Jill said, "No problem, I'll pay!" I then asked if she would like to drive up on Sunday to go skiing again. She agreed and we arranged a place to meet.

Riding a bicycle built for two around Stanley Park in Vancouver, B.C.

After six weeks of meeting at different locations for ice skating, swimming, and skiing, we finally decided that maybe I should pick her up at her house. The first time, I had trouble finding where she lived, and I was really running late. I finally stopped and called and, after getting better directions, I found her house and was introduced to her parents, Chet and Doris Johnson. Their home had a 20x40-foot swimming pool on the bluff of Puget Sound. No wonder she was such a good swimmer!

Our wedding day—October 5, 1963.

However, I learned the most about Jill and her family from Bob Larsen, a mutual friend and skiing buddy at Stevens Pass. Jill's parents were very nice and I was also introduced to the family dog, "Pokey," a schnauzer, who seemed to like me right away, which Jill said was unusual. We had many more ski dates that Winter and got to know each other all the better. We got engaged in August and were married on Oct. 5, 1963, only eight months after our first meeting. We were married in the Lutheran Church in the University District of Seattle, with mostly family and close friends attending. It was a rainy day, with a Husky football game going on only a block away at the same time, so traffic was horrible. Jill's parents hosted a dinner in their home after the wedding, and, in the evening, we had a reception for friends at the

Lakeside Gardens south of Everett, near Lake Serene, with a German band providing the music.

Our "puddle jumper"—1963 Volkswagen.

We had Jill's Volkswagen bug packed to the brim with camping and hunting gear for our honeymoon. Our first night was spent in a motel in north Everett, and the next night we stayed in Harrison Hot Springs in a rustic room. Then we traveled to the 100-mile post on the Alaskan Highway and camped along the lakes in Canada. From there, we headed east to Kamloops, Banff, and Glacier National Park. We then headed west again, hunting in the Blue Mountains of southeast Washington. We camped next to a water tank and, in the middle of the night, I heard an elk walking right next to our tent, which is the closest we got to an elk! Our two-week honeymoon was blessed with beautiful weather the whole time—a great way to begin our married life, which has lasted for 57 years as I write this. After our long trip, we were ready to move into our apartment in Kirkland, WA. We moved three times in the next two years, all in the same area.

My parents' home on Lake Michigan.

We took another long road trip to Michigan the following June to visit my family. Jill hadn't met my family, other than my mother and aunt Jean, who had come to visit us soon after we were engaged. We had a wonderful time visiting all my relatives, plus great days at their beach home right on Lake Michigan, with beautiful weather the whole time

The next Winter, we took another trip to Sun Valley for a week of skiing. Jill had just found out that she was pregnant, and we had a wonderful week of skiing. We were a day late getting back to work because our poor VW (we called it "Puddle-jumper") broke down in Boise, after making three long trips for us. But it was well worth the trip!

Our next project was to find a rental house with an extra bedroom, which we found in Kirkland.

Kristie meeting Kurt for the first time!

Chapter 11

Family Life

Jill was working in Payroll Department at the University of Washington, and I was working at Boeing in Renton. We were excited about having a baby, and the first thing we did was buy a crib. When it was delivered, the neighbors knew what was happening! Jill had an easy pregnancy and worked up until the delivery. We took pre-birth classes at the YMCA in Seattle and hoped we knew all about parenting a baby. She was two weeks overdue and finally was induced at Swedish Hospital in Seattle. Our beautiful daughter, Kristie, was born just after midnight on September 14, 1965. With my help in the delivery room, Jill had a fairly easy delivery and stayed in the hospital for the required three days. I brought them both home, spent one night, and went to her mother's house for several days—out of fear as to what to do with a baby. Her friend and neighbor, Colleen, said, "Don't worry, Mother Nature will tell you what to do." But it didn't happen that way for her. However, there were no problems and, after a few days, and Jill and the baby came home. At Christmas, when Kristie was three months old, my parents and brother, Tom, came out from Michigan to visit us and meet Kristie. We had a great week together.

Shortly afterward, I took a job at Western Gear Company, so we moved to a rental house in Everett. The next Summer, we found out we were going to have another addition to the family. In April, Kurt was born at Providence Hospital in Everett, after being two weeks overdue. My mother arrived a week before the due date and ended up staying almost a month, before she returned to Michigan. Our family was complete! I always wanted a son, and Jill and I agreed that if the second child wasn't a boy, we would keep having more babies! Thank you, Kurt, for being a boy! When Kurt was three months old, we found our dream house—to go along with our beautiful family.

Grandpa Fritz wanting to sneak Kristie into his suitcase and take her back to Michigan.

Kristie and Jill on Jill's parents' lawn in Edmonds.

Priest Point home (SE side, showing Swedish fireplace).

CHAPTER 12

Priest Point Living

JILL AND I HAD BEEN MARRIED FOR NEARLY FIVE YEARS, and, for the past two years, we had been looking to buy our own home, instead of renting. Kristie was almost two, and Kurt was a newborn. We had been looking for property and/or a home up north, in the Marysville/Arlington area of Washington. Jill needed her "nest!" I had a blank earnest-agreement form that I carried with me in case an owner agreed to sell the property or house. Shortly after this, I interviewed a congenial guy named Chris Kristad at the Western Gear Corporation. He told me that he lived at Priest Point, on the Tulalip Indian reservation. We walked outside and he pointed across the bay to where it was located. He mentioned that there were building lots for sale, and he explained to me how to get there. The following day, during my lunch hour, I drove out to Priest Point. After observing the building lots on Gays Drive, I turned onto Priest Point Drive and saw a For Sale sign. A nice home sat on a half-acre lot that overlooked Puget Sound. I was surprised that the grass hadn't been cut for some time. I became curious and knocked on the back door. The owner, Otto Olson, greeted me and invited me in. He explained that he and his wife, Pearl, had just returned from vacation. We entered the kitchen and my eyes immediately caught site of a semi-circular, Swedish-brick fireplace. It reminded me of a restaurant at Paw Paw Lake, near South Haven, that had four similar fireplaces. I used to take my prized dates there!

Right away, I became excited and Otto explained how it was designed. He said that every room in the house had a view—Mt. Rainier, the Mukilteo Lighthouse, and the Olympic and Cascade Mountains. I asked Otto if I could bring my wife over later that evening to see the house. He said it was okay to come around 6 p.m. We were warmly greeted by the couple when we arrived. It was just turning dusk when we looked out the picture window and saw a tug pulling a large log boom. The red and green lights were outlining the logs and reflecting onto the water. We learned that we had the same interests and hobbies as Otto and Pearl, especially gardening. As we were leaving, I asked Otto if I could back the next morning to see the Swedish fireplace in action, as he had said he always had a fire at 6 a.m. I arrived at the designated time and the fire warmed us as we talked about my employment manager position at Western Gear and other mutual interests, never bringing up buying the house.

Our Christmas picture when the kids were young.

Just before I left, Otto showed me the basement, and I could tell that the house was solidly built. He said that a Norwegian carpenter did the work and that Otto, himself, had handpicked the wood from the Weyerhaeuser mill, where he had worked as the shipping manager. After a pause in the conversation, I asked him what price he was asking for the house. I was assuming somewhere around $38,000. He said the price was $29,500. Not wanting to show my excitement, I asked him if he was willing to hold the contract. He paused for a moment and then agreed that he could do that. I asked at what interest, and he said 6%, which was equivalent to 3% in 2020. I then asked the duration of the loan, and he said 30 years. Finally, I asked how much money would be required for a down payment. He said $6,000.

All the while, I was restraining myself from showing too much interest. We walked upstairs and I told him I had a definite interest but only had $4,000 available for the down payment. Otto thought for a moment and said, if I could come up with another $2,000 in three months, that would work. I handed Otto the earnest agreement I had in my pocket, and he said he would take it to his attorney that day. We shook hands and I drove back to work. Later the same day, Otto called me and asked if I was sure that I wanted to go through with the sale. I said that I definitely was sure. He said he'd get the paperwork completed and set up a date for signatures. Later, I found out that his son was a financial officer at Everett Trust and Savings bank. I assumed that he tried to talk Otto out of selling the house.

In the interceding months, Jill and the kids and I would take our old, wooden boat out into Port Gardner Bay and cross over to Priest Point, just far enough to see our "soon-to-become" home. Before long, money became a challenge. We sold our camper and a few other things. Then, just one week before final closing we still were $1,000 short. That weekend we parked our 1962 Volkswagen bug in the Pay 'n Save parking lot, and on Saturday a man bought it for his son, who needed transportation for college. The next Thursday, we met at the lawyer's office and signed the preliminary paperwork. Later that month, the closing process was complete, and the house was ours!

Since Otto and Pearl hadn't moved that far away, we saw a lot of them over the years. Otto had a huge workshop, woodshed, and garage on the property. Since he had lots of tools that he was sorting out after moving, he would come to visit often. He would help us with the garden and show me how to prune the trees and shrubs. Buying that house was one of the very best things we ever did in life, and we are so thankful to Otto and Pearl for selling it to us. We remained best friends with them until their final days. Otto died of cancer in a hospital, but he never told Pearl what he was suffering from, as he didn't want to burden her.

The kids on the toboggan with their babysitter.

Our budget was very tight. I was on a monthly salary, with no overtime, even though I worked 10-hour days, six days a week, keeping all of Western Gear's jobs filled. The house came with a 60x60-foot garden, had 100 lineal feet of raspberries, gooseberries, logan berries, quince berries, four apple trees, a plum tree, a pear tree and six flowering cherry trees. And we had three miles of beach, where we would have picnic dinners and I could fish for cutthroat trout and salmon. We also had our boat, with a five-horsepower motor, so we could drop our crab pots and motor over to Camano Island for clams for more good eating. Since we moved into the house in August—with the garden that was left to us and the seafood from Puget Sound, we literally were eating off the land!

One of our early family Christmas cards.

Having sold the Volkswagen, our second car, to buy the house, Jill was left without transportation and relied on neighbors to get around during the week. I remember her going to the grocery store once a month (since I was on a monthly salary) to buy the necessary items. We bought a used box freezer from a neighbor, Muriel, who was selling her home, so we could freeze items needed for the next month. We bought fresh eggs from the Bradys, which was a nice walk from our house though the holly fields, as we called them, which gave Jill and the kids an outing. And the milkman delivered our milk on the doorstep twice a week. Jill's dad gave us his old rototiller; that next Spring, I rototilled and planted our first garden. The Bradys had accumulated years of chicken manure, so I drove our 1953 Ford pickup to their property, filled up the bed, and spread it over the garden area and rototilled it into the soil. We had a beautiful garden that year. Jill inherited her mother's pressure cooker, and she learned to can vegetables, fruits, jams, and juices. The basement cupboard was filled to the brim!

Kurt and Kristie with Santa Claus.

The next year, we made our own sauerkraut with our great German neighbor, Dorothy Richardson, who was a real pro at it. We inherited a cabbage shredder from Jill's uncle Frank. And we had a four-foot-long wooden plunger that we used to shred and pound the cabbage in the crocks. Dorothy was very good at measuring the right amount of salt for each crock. We carried on the sauerkraut tradition for many years. After Dorothy passed away, our new neighbors and good friends, Gene and Pauline Lindahl, helped us make it every year. They would shred the cabbage, and Gene and I would take turns pounding it. We all drank beer and sang German songs as we worked. One time, after the crocks were filled, Gene and I were wheelbarrowing the crocks up to Gene's house to be stored in his basement. Apparently, too much beer caused the wheelbarrow to tip, and we broke one of the crocks that was filled to the top! Bad idea!

We also had fun making apple cider with our good friends, the Laurens. They had an antique apple press, and we had so many apples that we would put everyone to work making cider. And we learned to make our own wines in five-gallon carboy containers, since we had so many raspberries. The kids became very helpful in stomping the berries barefoot in a huge tub, from which the juice flowed into a strainer and the large carboys. We became so successful that we began making blackberry and grape wines, too. I eventually built a sandbox and had a swing set built for the kids. The 800-square-foot basement was unfurnished. In the Winter, the kids would ride their Big Wheels in the basement, where they couldn't hurt anything. From upstairs, you could hear them banging into the furnace and the sideboards. They had a riding horse they both used all the time, but we kept that upstairs so we could keep our eyes on them. Our new young neighbors, Lynn and Bill Noel, were about Kristie's and Kurt's ages and used to come and play a lot. Their mother, Sandy, and Jill would take turns every week giving one of them a "get away" for the day, while the other watched all the kids. Eventually, more kids moved into the neighborhood, and Jill would earn extra money watching the kids at our house.

Just before Gene and Pauline's landscaping was done and the rockery placed on a steep slope on the water/road side of their house, we used to get the toboggan and go out and play at night, after the kids had gone to bed. While one of us watched the road for cars, the other shoved the riders off down the steep hill. We heard them laughing all the way down, until they crashed into a burn barrel at the bottom of the long hill, which saved them from going over the 40-foot bluff into Puget Sound. They destroyed the burn barrel but saved themselves!

After several years, we found that artificial fertilizers just didn't produce the vegetables in the garden like the real stuff. Jill was excited when she and a neighbor, Rusty Wilson, heard about free chicken manure in a town near Marysville. Her husband, Sim, was owner of the local newspaper, called *The Globe*. Rusty borrowed his old van that he used to distribute the paper each week. I had just finished rototilling the garden, when the van pulled into our garden area. Jill and Rusty jumped from the van and looked at me. I asked, " Where's the chicken manure?" I could detect a foul odor emanating from inside the van. Jill opened the back door, grabbed the shovel, ran to me, and cried a horrified, guttural tone, "Heeerrreee—you shovel it!" The manure was piled in the bed of the van. I shoveled the slimy, ripe chicken manure onto the ground; you could smell it two blocks away. Poor Sim had his van towed to the wrecking yard after that adventure. It had performed its last duty!

When Kristie was four years old, she was very shy. Jill suggested that, if she had another car, we could get her involved in a nursery school. I bought her a 1953 Ford sedan that we called "Old Smokey," as it always burned lots of oil. It was a great savior for both kids and Jill. Kurt always was very outgoing and had no problems with socializing. Surprisingly, as the kids got older, it was just the opposite with their personalities—Kristie had become very outgoing and Kurt more quiet. Jill's mother paid for dancing classes in Everett for Kristie to help her come out of her shyness. Kurt had a ball playing with the other kids his age, while waiting for the classes to be over. One of the other mothers talked about a dog they had that was causing problems in the neighborhood where they lived, as he was a chicken killer! She showed Jill pictures of the dog they called "Tippy," because the ends of his ears had black hair. He was a white-haired, cockapoo mix (but a mutt) and was cute. He was waiting in her car. And since she said they needed to find him a new home, Jill loaded him up and brought him home, not sure of what I would say. When I got home that night, the dog came and sat right by my feet, looked up at me with sad eyes, as if saying, "May I stay?" He turned out to be a great dog for the family for the next 14 years. However, we did change his name to Tipps.

With the kids and Tipps at the Johnson pool.

A great day of hunting in Tenino!

Chapter 13

Life in Olympia

WHEN WE FIRST MOVED TO OLYMPIA, the capital of Washington state, we lived on a small farm with horses, which was close to Mud Bay on southern Puget Sound. The owners of the home were moving to Kentucky, so they would be putting the house up for sale. They arranged for us to paint the house, inside and out, plus the barn and other out buildings, rent free. We lived there for six months and moved when school let out. We couldn't move into a house in town for a couple of weeks, so we moved out to Millersylvania State Park and camped out. Jill, the kids and Tipps were sleeping in a tent, and I slept in the back of our Barracuda car, since I had to be at work the next day. On the first night, Tipps woke up to see a skunk near the tent and gave chase. He got sprayed very badly and made his way back into the tent! Needless to say, everyone got out of the tent in a hurry, and I was awakened by their screams. No one got much sleep the rest of the night. Jill and the kids spent the next couple of days washing him with tomato juice in the lake, away from all the other campers.

We finally were able to move into a Cape Cod-style duplex that had lots of room. The kids went to an elementary school that had an "open concept" arrangement. A school bus would pick them up in front of the house. After a couple of years, Jill began working for the Olympia Police Department, and the kids became very responsible for getting on the bus by themselves. The next-door neighbor also would watch for them after school and make sure they were OK. Kurt was active in soccer, and Kristie was a Campfire Girl.

Picking wild flowers in Tenino.

Olympia was a great place to live, as it was a step away from the ocean, the mountains, Puget Sound, and state parks. I worked a 4/10 week, so we had three-day weekends and would take long trips to get out of town. I often would go pheasant hunting at Scatter Creek, south of Olympia. Tipps was my hunting dog, and we often would end up with more birds than the hunters with pedigree dogs. Jill and the kids sometimes would go with me as an outing. One day, after hunting, we drove to Tenino a small town south of Olympia. While Jill was at the park with the kids, I went to a tavern for a beer and met the greatest guy, Earl Blodgett, who owned 200 acres of property at the end of a valley. He and his wife, Iola, had been dairy farmers in Oregon and just recently moved to Tenino. He was happy to meet someone local. He immediately invited us out to visit them and said I could hunt all I wanted on his property. We became very good friends and had wonderful times together. Earl loved going to auctions and buying and selling animals.

One day, he bought two small ponies for our kids to ride. They had a couple of milk cows and chickens, so we always bought a gallon or two of milk, at $1 gallon, and fresh eggs. The milk had about two inches of thick cream on top, so Jill learned to make butter and lots of homemade ice cream. One Saturday, I went out by myself and hunted for pheasants in the morning and deer in the afternoon on Earl's property. I came home with two birds and a 200-pound, blacktail deer. We would have Earl and Iola come to town and have dinner with us quite often. Jill and Iola loved to go thrift-store shopping, while Earl and I drank beer and swapped stories. We kept track of them until their dying days, as they always would get the yearning to move to properties that they could fix up and sell in different cities and states. They both had so much energy.

Kurt and his pony.

In 1971, I left Washington Natural Gas and we had moved to Olympia for the Washington State Parks job. Fortunately for us, we were able to rent our house at Priest Point to our neighbors, the Estensons, whose house had just burned down. In 1976, I began work on the Alaska pipeline in Prudhoe Bay and once again we moved back to Priest Point. We lived there until 2000, when we moved to Jill's parents' penthouse and lived there the next 20 year, then once again moved back to Priest Point.

A good day of crabbing.

Chapter 14

Return to Priest Point

THE KIDS WERE HAPPY TO BE back in their old neighborhood, and Tipps was happy to be able to roam wherever he wanted! It was a miracle that he survived living in Olympia, because our house was on a busy street and he wasn't that smart about cars. It was a very sad day when we had to put Tipps down, as he was having problems with his prostate. Neither Jill nor I could hold him as they gave him his final shot. We should have had the kids there to help! After that, we said no more dogs, as it was too hard to lose them. But—guess what? Gene told us there was a nice looking stray dog in the neighborhood that was going to be shot by a neighbor soon, as he kept getting into garbage cans. We went for a walk the next night and saw him, and we didn't talk to him, but he followed us home anyway. I told Kristie and Jill not to feed him or talk to him, but apparently they did anyway. So we adopted another dog, who we named Duke and who turned out to be a wonderful companion for the next 15 years. He was just a young dog when he came to live with us, and he never got over getting into garbage cans, even though he was well-fed. He also was very spoiled. I never wanted to get him neutered, so he would wander off, sometimes for days, if another dog was in heat. We would have to go find him and drag him home. I finally relented and had him fixed.

Kristie on Skyhawk in our front yard at Priest Point.

Kristie enjoyed her two different horses, "Skyhawk," an Indian Paint and "Mischief," an Appaloosa, at two different times. She joined enjoyed 4-H and showed them in competition. At her first Washington State Fair showing, she looked very pretty in her western attire, and Skyhawk was groomed to perfection. All the horses were lined up, waiting for the competition to begin. Unbeknownst to us, Kristie was very nervous at this point. The next thing we knew, she dropped the reins and slid to the ground. Skyhawk looked down at her and put his head on her shoulder, as if to ask, "What's wrong. What do I do now?" Some nice person helped Kristie to her feet, but she was then disqualified and had to leave the arena. However, she became very comfortable showing after that experience.

Kurt had a motorized dirt bike that he enjoyed for a time, but he then proceeded to tear the whole machine apart to try to fix something! Once, while riding near our house in the holly fields, he fell, the bike fell on top of him, and he was pinned under it. He yelled for help and a neighbor came to his rescue. Both kids were involved with sports all their school years. Kristie lettered in cross-country running, tennis, track, and soccer. And Kurt was involved in swimming, basketball, and soccer.

Kurt on his motorbike.

Duke on look-out at the beach!

Westerly view of Puget Sound from our penthouse apartment in Edmonds.

Chapter 15

Penthouse Living

WE STAYED IN OUR HOME FOR the next 20 wonderful years. Both Kristie and Kurt had graduated from high school and moved out by then. In 1990, we approached Jill's parents about buying their apartment that they were going to put on the market. They agreed and we moved into the penthouse and rented out the house again.

As it worked out, we lived in the penthouse for the next 20 years, being next door to her parents, as they aged and needed assistance. Duke was not too happy living in a fenced-in deck in the penthouse, as he could smell the low tide and wasn't able to get to it. I finally had him neutered, as he was constantly barking and trying to escape. We enjoyed him for many more years, but finally his days were limited. Kristie, Jill, and I loaded him into the back of the station wagon and drove to the local veterinary, where they administered a shot as we all talked to him, hugged him and cried! After Duke's passing, I wrote this poem-like summary about him:

"*We learned one evening that Duke was there. An orphan dog that came from somewhere. He followed us home and was there in the morning to everyone's delight. I came home from work and everyone asked, 'Can we keep him, Dad?' Up on his hips but down on his front legs, he looked up at me and asked to be one of us. How could I turn down those pleading brown eyes? OK, I said, you fed him last night, he's part of the family now. He learned quickly not to chew on the chairs,* books, and shoes and that the salmon on the counter was not for him to eat. He loved the beach and could smell the low tide. He'd go down and chase fish in the small pools of water for hours on end and always knew to come back home when the tide came in. When I was away in Saudi Arabia, he took up the slack of a devoted companion until I came back. No one knows from where he came. We are all so glad that God brought him for us to love. Now we're returning his remains to the place where he was so happy. We know he's up above chasing the fish. We'll always keep the memories of his love."

One of the 4th of July celebrations with extended family and friends.

We enjoyed those two decades we lived in the penthouse. After work in the Summer, we all went swimming at 5 p.m. and then had cocktails on the deck. Quite a few neighbors would come and join us in the pool. Jill's dad had his 10-foot Livingstone boat anchored in the bay out front of their house. We would put out the crab pots and pull them the next day. We had many crab feeds and dinners for family, friends, and neighbors over the years. Sometimes, I would go for a bike ride, instead of swimming. Every Saturday night was steak night, and we would take turns cooking. Jill's brother, Dave, and his wife,

Inge, lived right next door, so they would do it one week, her parents another week, and Jill and I the third week. On most Sunday's, we'd have a joint dinner with our combined four children and four grandchildren. And there always was a Fourth of July celebration, with extended family and friends.

One of our Sunday dinners with the Johnson clan.

In 2010, Jill's parents died within four months of each other—her dad was 102 and her mother, 94. Shortly after they died, we drove up to our Priest Point home, as the last renters had just moved out. We looked at each other and said, "Let's move back." We were so excited! After repainting, we put carpet over all the wood floors. We updated the kitchen several years later as well as the master bathroom. Otto would be unhappy that we took out his pink-and-gray tile!

Chapter 16

Building Heavy Machinery

In 1966, I became the employment manager in Western Gear's Heavy Machinery Division in Everett. The division manufactured wenches for ships, logging equipment, and custom cargo-loading systems. The division consisted of the fabrication, machine shop, and final-assembly sections. When the division won a government contract, like to build an underwater-cable-laying system, I would advertise for fitters and welders and fill the jobs in a month, while at the same time filling all other openings in the division. I also was responsible for recruiting engineering graduates from the University of Washington, Washington State University, and other institutions around the country.

In 1967, the Boeing Company was building the first giant 747 airliners at its new factory, also in Everett. Western Gear's Heavy Machinery Division was awarded the contract for design and fabrication of the cargo-loading system. As employment manager, I recruited nationwide for every department head in the new Cargo-Loading Division. My experience as a prior employee of Boeing helped immensely. I spent weekends at the office and at home in the evenings calling and interviewing. I also set up tests for selection of manufacturing employees. While all of these things were going on, the division was trying to fend off a movement to unionize the professional and salaried personnel. The company had changed its benefits programs without informing the employees. I had the responsibility to give presentations of the new programs to all of the employees.

The manufacturing employees already were in the Metal Trades Union. When the vote on unionization for all other employees was held, they voted not to have union representation I also had secondary duties, like being one of the United Way representatives for Snohomish County, while at the same time taking care of the United Way signup of employees. I formed a committee of two employees from each department that doubled the company contributions in the first year. I also organized all of the employee sports activities, including the dinners for the trophy presentations in each sport. And I made job evaluations and comparative wage and salary calculations. I was working 50 to 60 hours a week, with no overtime pay and very little reward for accomplishing my written objectives. One day, I asked the general manager, "How important is it to have all the machines operating, especially the three-million-dollar NC milling machine?" He replied that human-resource people are a dime a dozen! The company was family owned by the Bannon family, who followed the same unfair and insensitive principles.

Chapter 17

Washington Natural Gas Company

IN 1966, I MOVED ON TO the Washington Natural Gas Company as assistant to the safety/training director. Most of my duties were managing the company training for the Seattle, Bellevue, and Everett Divisions. I also filled in for the employment manager when he was out of town. And I conducted the American Management Association courses in supervision, the customer-service qualification course for technicians, the welding-qualification course for fabricators, the instrumentation course for engineers, and a program that I developed for all employees titled, "Your Company in Action," which took a year and a half to design. I handed out a form to employees in each operating unit, asking their main objective and an overall description of their activities. After collecting this information, I took photos of the employees performing their work and made a storyboard for each activity. Then I wrote a narrative to accompany the slide presentation. I asked an employee, who also was a part-time actor, to record the voiceover for the slide show. The program was given to all the employees and used for the orientation of new employees.

I also worked closely with the standards manager to produce a guide book for non-company installers. I was responsible for assigning newly hired professional people that various departments needed to accomplish their work. On one memorable occasion, a customer was upset with something and forwarded her complaint to the federal

Handing out reports to staff at the Washington Gas Company.

government. Somehow, the complaint, addressed to the president of the Washington Natural Gas Company, reached President Richard Nixon. I was immediately given the task of finding someone to lead a seminar in customer courtesy. All 600 employees attended the seminar. [Unfortunately, the customer had a natural malcontent personality, as the company had a good record of customer service.] I was very active in the Society for Training and Development and served on different interview panels. One of the panels involved selection of the King County training director. I enjoyed working for Avery Willis, who was the director of safety and training. He was one of the best supervisors I ever worked for. The last year that I worked for Washington Natural Gas Company, I coordinated 100,000 man hours of training.

Chapter 18

Washington State Parks and Recreation

LATER IN 1971, I WAS HIRED as training officer for the Washington State Parks and Recreation Department. The step was a big one because it meant uprooting my wife and two children, renting our Marysville home, and moving to Olympia. I was responsible for career development for all employees, participated in hiring and training park rangers, and coordinated the supervisory development courses throughout the state. I conducted Train the Trainer courses that gave park rangers the tools to develop their own presentations. And I originated a federal-grant application for the cross-training of federal, state, and county park rangers. As project director, I had to determine the training needs, make assessments, and estimate the cost of transporting the trainees to Port Townsend, WA, where they stayed in the former officers' quarters at Fort Warden State Park. The results saved money by sharing resources.

I was fortunate to take advantage of the many courses offered by the State Central Training Division. I wrote policies and procedures for the Personnel Department, which were approved by my boss, the agency personnel manager. Once a month, the training officers from all of the state departments would meet and share ideas for new training programs. And I attended supervisory-development programs at various other agencies, retrieving information that was useful in our agency.

At my desk in the Washington State Parks Department office.

In 1975, funding for my position expired, so during the time off, I enrolled at the Evergreen State College in Olympia for a degree in Safety Program Management, paid for by my GI Bill. At the same time, I was assigned to the Security Department at Evergreen, with responsibility for formulating a safety policy. Since the college was new and little work had gone into a formal safety program, I asked the State Department of Labor and Industries to come in and make a safety survey of the different sections. They did a thorough job of what needed to be accomplished. I then wrote procedures for how to implement these recommendations. Another of my duties was investigating accidents.

About to board the Grumman Goose with Jill in Alaska.

Chapter 19

Building the Alaska Pipeline

ONE FRIDAY EVENING IN OLYMPIA, our phone rang. The caller was the owner of the Alaska General Construction Company, offering me a job. He had contacted a recruiter I used to work with when I was employment manager at Western Gear. Since I had previous safety experience at Washington Natural Gas and had added safety-programming management to my background, it aligned with his immediate need for a safety engineer in Prudhoe Bay, AK. I asked him if I could think it over. He replied, "You have until Sunday to decide. I want you to fly up Monday morning and begin the job immediately." He said I would work for five weeks, then fly home for one week of rest and relaxation (R&R) in Olympia, and then fly back to Alaska. I talked to Jill, and we agreed that I should accept the offer. On Sunday, I packed my things and, the next morning, Jill and the kids drove me to Sea-Tac Airport. The 747 airliner was packed with guys headed to Anchorage to work on the Alaska pipeline. The airplane was heavily loaded with the workers' tools and equipment. Using full take-off power, the plane barely made it off the end of the runway.

The next day in Anchorage, I was given a physical examination and issued heavy Arctic clothing. I then stopped to talk to the people who I would be coordinating with between Prudhoe Bay and Anchorage. The next morning, I boarded a Wien Alaska 737. Sitting near me was the president of Alaska General Construction. He greeted me and the other workers. The flight attendant was the most attractive Native-American young lady I've ever seen. It was a beautiful, sunshiny day. We flew over Mt. McKinley, along the Brooks Range mountains, and landed in Prudhoe Bay. It was August and, much to my surprise, there was mud everywhere. The construction site had been excavated, and it had rained afterwards. The office manager met me at the airport and took me to a large complex of double-wide trailers all joined together. My room was 12 feet long and 10 feet wide. Different roommates would come and go, so you never knew who the next one would be or where in the United States he would be from. A central furnace supplied heat for two rooms. After every 10-hour day, the rooms became happy-hour locations for beer, hard liquor, and pot. These parties helped to offset the fatigue and stress from the 10-hour shifts, seven days a week. Most workers drank liquor. I drank Lipton diet iced tea with saccharin, which often resulted in me dancing and singing, "I'm not the plumber, but I'm the plumber's son." The huge cafeteria fed 1,400 employees. There was no shortage of steak, lobster, fish, and other exotic dishes. On future trips north, I always brought a bottle of vodka to drink before Thursday steak. After a while, the workers became tired of expensive foods and requested milkshakes, hamburgers, and French fries.

One Friday evening, a band played and we held a dance. Since we mostly were men, we danced independently. There were only three of these dance sessions, headed by an older lady, who was the entertainment director. Every evening after dinner, three movies were shown. During the Summers, the sun shown 22 hours a day. I would sometimes go to the first movie at 8:30 p.m., see two more movies, and go outside at 3 a.m. to bright sunshine. When I was on my R&R, I always brought back lots of books that kept me occupied. There was an exercise building next door to my office, where I would go several times a day, working mostly on the rowing machine. Volleyball games were played inside the large storage building. During Winter, we would run inside the Arctic walkway, through the snow, and into and around the storage building.

Shortly after I arrived, I found out why Alaska General needed an on-site safety engineer in such a hurry. Two carpenters had fallen from rooftops at different times within days of each other, landing on their heads. Another construction worker had a heart attack and was temporarily put into the carpentery shack and left unattended, while the infirmary was only a few hundred feet away. He died at the end of the day.

I had to take immediate steps to slow down these occurrences. I developed a "Notification of Corrective Action" form. The top part of the form was my assessment of unsafe conditions that I found throughout the work areas and what was needed to correct them. The bottom of the form stated the "Corrective Action Taken." The forms were given to the construction manager, who would see that the corrective actions were carried out and that a copy was sent to me.

I had a company truck and drove to every work site in Prudhoe Bay. I soon became well acquainted with all the supervisors. There were 14 different crafts working within a 10-mile radius of Arco's Heavy Operations and Maintenance facility. When I arrived in August of 1975, there was a frenzy of earth-moving activity, to beat the onset of cold weather. The water mains, sewer pipes, electrical hookups, and cement foundations all had to be completed before the ground froze. Then, the building frameworks had to be erected for the large, modular buildings that were on their way from Seattle on barges, and roads had to be built. It was crucial that an open channel be maintained through the Arctic ice in the Beaufort Sea, so the tugs pulling the barges could make it through to the Arco drilling site. Everyone was happy to see the barges arrive and to then watch the huge cranes lift the buildings from the barges onto the huge, diesel-powered hauling vehicles, for transport to the various oilfield locations. An entire gymnasium building was transported and placed in the main Arco complex.

Profanity runs deep in the heavy-construction-worker culture. The f---word was used in almost every sentence. The majority of these workers came from large U.S. cities in the East. They were hardcore and tough. One day, I approached a steel worker and asked him to put on his hard hat. His reply was, "I'm not gonna do it, and I'll knock your head off if you try to make me do it!" My reply was, "Go ahead and try." He put on his hard hat. Later, I found out that he had been a professional fighter. Soon after that, he was fired for breaking the nose of a co-worker. Another incident I experienced later was even more threatening. A new work-scheduling person was hired and assigned to my room. I observed that he had a numerous assortment of pills. The first week, at exactly 10 p.m., he would tell me to turn off my music so he could sleep. I would oblige. One night, he asked again. At 10:02 p.m., I said I only had a few minutes left on a tape from my family. I was lying in bed when he jumped up, hovered over me, and yelled, "I'll kill you!" I didn't panic, and replied, "I'll get up and turn the player off." He sat back down on his bed. I got up, turned the player off, stepped into the hallway, and said "OK, dammit, come out here and see if you think can do it!" Evidently, he wasn't as tough as he thought he was, and was afraid he might lose his job. He then walked down the hallway to the assistant production manager's room. Unbeknown to him, the assistant manager could tell that he was a druggie. I slept in a different room that night. The next day, he was fired and sent back to the states. Working in that culture was adventurous, and you could not let obnoxious workers stand in your way!

After a couple of months of being a strict disciplinarian with the construction workers, I decided to include some humor. The larger fabrication work was housed in a gymnasium-type building. One day, I came in dancing and singing my "Plumbers" routine. I danced over to a ladder and climbed up to a balcony, where I looked down at the men below. I shouted down to them, held out my right arm and shouted, "Heil Hitler!" Then I gave a short speech in German-gibberish-like syllables. All the men below responded with "Heil Hitler" salutes. Every day, I would come and we would go through the same routine. One day, as I approached the door, Clancy, a lead boilermaker, abruptly stopped me and said, "Don't go in there now. There are a number of Arco big shots with reporters taking pictures. I quickly exited and was saved!

Happy Hour in the rooms became the time for dirty-joke telling and other men-type amusements. Bill, a chubby, red-faced Teamster said, "It's so cold out there that my prick turned into a toothpick!" There was only one female employee, and she was the girlfriend of the assistant construction manager. She sometimes attended our Happy-Hour sessions. Of course, we had to tone down our language when she was there. Any time a female was hired, she had a boyfriend working for the company; everyone respected the legitimacy of those relationships. There also were cleaning women, who changed the sheets and kept the rooms and building in respectable condition.

About my third month on site, I conducted an all-skills training committee meeting. We had a great exchange of ideas and incorporated new and better safety standards throughout the construction site. Unfortunately, after a while, the meetings became "bitching" sessions, with few safety implementations.

About the seventh month, the workers agreed that they needed an additional dining building. They decided that the first group that was served would stay longer and force the rest to wait and not come in. Somehow, their plan leaked out to the construction project manager. The next day, Security identified 300 people who remained seated at dinner, forcing the others to wait. Two 737s were pulled up outside the cafeteria, because Security wanted to fire the agitators and quickly load them onto the planes before they opened their liquor bottles. However, this didn't stop them from drinking.

The first 737 was almost loaded, when a forklift driver accidentally punctured the plane's fuelage. They tried to get the last passenger onto the stairway of the plane, but he saw the holes in the side of the plane and ran up the stairway shouting, "The plane's gonna crash!" This caused a stampede of drunks—and probably druggies—off of the plane. Quick-thinking guards put them onto a bus and drove four miles to the other landing strip and herded them onto another airplane. The airplane with the holes took off and landed at the same airfield and loaded the second group of workers aboard. Luckily, none of them saw the holes. The airplane took off, flew at a lower attitude, and landed at Anchorage. The workers were on 12-week R&R cycles, resulting in numerous divorces and breakups from their wives/girlfriends. There also were a lot of faked injuries, which enabled them to fly back to the Lower 48 and resolve their relationships.

My R&R cycle seemed like a long five weeks between visits home. My first flight home, I grabbed a milk flight out of Prudhoe Bay at 2 a.m. and landed at Sea-Tac at 10 a.m. I arrived in Olympia at our duplex and immediately called Jill at the Olympia Police Department, where she worked. She said, "I'll be right home for lunch." We didn't have all that much time for lunch! When Jill walked back into the police department, one of the officers said, "Smile, if you got a little!" She did smile—and laughed.

Boarding the plane to fly home for R&R.

What could have been an end to my life was the beginning of one of my R&R trips home. At midnight, the bus drove out to the Dead Horse Airport tarmac. There were 60 people waiting to board a Wien Alaska 737 cargo/passenger plane. It was an especially cold night. The airplane's front cargo-loading sections were being filled with 10-foot-long steel cylinders. Looking out the airport window, I could see the icy surfaces glistening like thousands of diamonds. Eventually, we all were seated in the rear section of the plane. A partition separated the front cargo area from the rear passenger section. We fastened our seat belts and settled back into our seats. The pilot of the heavily loaded airplane sped down the runway, revved up the engines, and left the ground. Just as the plane was reaching maximum takeoff power, there was a loud rumbling inside the cargo area. The entire partition broke apart, and the iron cylinders came sliding toward us. We all raised our feet to deflect them. The flight attendant leaped on top of the man sitting next to me. At that moment, the pilot immediately changed the control surfaces (flaps, ailerons, rudder and horizontal stabilizer controls) to control the added weight in the back of the airplane. He also banked, which slid the cylinder sideways under the passenger seats. When the aircraft leveled off, the co-pilot came aft, and we all worked to lash the cylinders to the seats. After a smooth landing in Fairbanks, we all cheered and clapped for the pilot. He did an extraordinary job and saved us all from death! Most of the Wien pilots were former "bush" pilots, with military-combat experience. The 737s were designed for short landing fields in remote areas of the world. It was an exciting feeling when they would swoop down through the clouds and touch down for a landing.

Shortly after arriving at Prudhoe Bay, a fire destroyed the new sewage-treatment plant. Welders torched through a composite blanket that surrounded a large filtering system. I was driving on the other side of the camp when I heard about the fire. I sped to the site, but no one was hurt. Afterward, I developed a form that had to be filled out prior to any welding or cutting. Another time, I had to monitor a gas-line repair in the gas-turbine building. There were no shut-off valves available and no way to make the modifications, except to unscrew the piping and place the new valves. Because natural gas explodes when the air mixture is between eight and 11 percent carbon dioxide, it was necessary to place portable fans next to the workers. I worked all night long with an explosive meter to make sure the upper and lower percentages remained in the non-explosive ranges. At one point, a wrench fell onto the floor, which could have caused a spark. We all were relieved when the job was finished. I used the explosive meter all around the construction site to identify any possible leaks inside enclosed areas.

One morning, 30 workers were building an Arctic walkway. A large crane was hoisting heavy beams and large piping from the ground over and down to the walkway. At 10:30 a.m., just after the workers left for their morning break, the flywheel on the crane broke, causing the boom to come crashing down where the workers had just been. The crane's periodic inspections were not up-to-date. After that, we used a different heavy-equipment supplier. Another incident occurred when four employees were sent to a drilling site, where pile drivers had just finished pounding down four steel pilings. The pipes pierced the permafrost and decaying peat moss, where methane gas had formed. The welders were welding metal connecting plates to a concrete slab. The pipes had a combustible mixture of methane and air, which exploded, lifting the concrete slab three feet off the ground. The four men were thrown backwards and landed on the ground, but no one was hurt. I talked to the site engineer, suggesting that we fill the pipes with concrete. We followed this procedure on the rest of the equipment-support applications.

Warmer weather brought the sunshine back, and the tundra turned from brown to thousands of multicolored flowers and shrubs. Ducks, geese, and terns returned. Every day, caribou would walk through the camp. Many times, I could reach out and touch them. The Arctic foxes that were white in the Winter transformed to their rusty red in the Spring. Brown bears came out of hibernation. Occasionally, you would hear the cook banging pans to keep them away from the kitchen. The little marmots that had hibernated under the snow suddenly began appearing in the carpentry shacks. Suddenly, rivers and streams flowed down from the Brooks Range, passing near the construction site. We cast our fishing lines into the streams, but unfortunately, I never caught any fish. On warm days, I enjoyed walking along the railroad tracks that lay between our camp and the Atlantic Richfields facilities. The tracks bisected a marsh, where sea gulls and terns built their nests. The terns resented my presence and would fly at my head, making me duck to avoid them. Finally, I decided to throw stones at them. I never hit any, but when the stones came close to them, they seemed aware of the potential danger and kept clear.

The Prudhoe Bay site bordered the Beaufort Sea. The water was crystal clear and the bottom was covered with small, multi-colored stones. One day, my friend, Jay Leque, and I drove a mile from camp to see a brown bear. Several trucks already were parked in the area. We looked down a hillside to where the bear was sleeping. He had just gorged himself on a dead caribou. Several men wanted pictures of the bear in action, so they began throwing stones at it. They were crazy, because a brown bear can run faster than a racehorse! But they made it back to their trucks safely.

Kristie and Kurt ready to hit the slopes at Crystal Mountain.

Since I was gone five weeks at a time, Jill and the kids took a ski bus up Crystal Mountain, where they all took ski lessons. It was a great getaway for them. Both Kristie and Kurt turned into excellent skiers and they continued to take the ski bus in junior high school, once we moved back to Marysville. Since we couldn't afford for all four of us to buy ski-lift tickets, Jill and I took up cross-country skiing, which we enjoyed as much as downhill. On one of my week-long leaves, we had a great time Spring skiing in Sun Valley with friends and their children.

In the late summer of 1976, as the Alaska-pipeline project was nearing completion, I decided that I wanted to return to Washington state to be with my wife and kids. I called Jill and asked her to meet me in Fairbanks and take a vacation trip back to our family home back in Tulalip. Jill arranged for the children to stay with her parents for a week. After she arrived, we took a riverboat tour to an Indian village, then toured the University of Alaska, where they grew cabbage that were huge! The next day, we boarded a train for Mt. McKinley National Park. That night we slept in a converted Pullman sleeping car. Next morning, we boarded a bus and toured the park, sighting mountain sheep, black bears, and caribou. Next day, a train took us through the mountains and into Anchorage.

We found lodging and rented a compact car for a drive down the Kenai Peninsula. While in Anchorage, we toured the ruins of the 1964 earthquake, looking down the hillsides that once were level ground. We visited several pubs and settled for a soup-and-salad dinner. The next morning, we drove to the town of Homer on the Kenai Peninsula. We stopped along the ocean and watched the Indians pulling in their nets full of silver salmon. We drove into town and noticed hundreds of sport fishermen landing silver salmon with almost every cast into the Kenai River. I tried to rent or buy a fishing rod, but there were none available. I had asked Jill to bring my pole from home, but she couldn't figure out how to get it on the plane and what we would do with the salmon if we caught some. I still talk about her not bringing the pole, but I've finally forgiven her after 57 years!

We drove over to the east side of the Kenai Peninsula to see the glaciers. The hillsides were full of beautiful, red fireweed. Upon returning to town, we found that there were no rooms available. So we had a nice dinner at the historic Driftwood Inn Hotel and returned to our small car and tried to sleep. Eventually, we ended up sleeping outside under a picnic table. It's a good thing the weather was fairly warm and dry! The next day, we headed back to Anchorage and made arrangements to ferry back to Seattle, through the inside passage. It was necessary to first fly from Anchorage to Juneau and catch a flight north to Haines. We took off, climbed up over the Chugach Mountains, and followed the coast into Juneau. Afterward, we visited a popular local tourist tavern, with sawdust on the floor. Then we went to the airport and waited to board a 10-passenger Grumman Goose amphibian, propeller airplane.

We noticed a heavyset Native Alaskan woman waiting to board the plane with her mother, and we could tell she was very drunk. Soon afterward, Jill and I boarded the airplane and we sat down and tightened our seat belts. We heard a commotion as other Indians were helping the drunken lady onto the airplane and into her seat. The pilot taxied the plane for takeoff and revved the two engines to full throttle. The aged plane began rattling, bumping, and weaving. At once, the drunken lady became hysterical and screamed, "Let me out of here, let me out of here!" A couple of other passengers tried to keep her quiet. The rattling and bumping continued as the airplane reached full takeoff power. Jill and I both wondered if we would get airborne before the plane broke apart. Finally, the pilot reduced engine power and the plane flew right over the Wrangell National Park. It was a beautiful sight as he made a circle, even with the drunken woman screaming all the way!

We looked down at the water, islands, lakes, and rivers as we flew north. After an hour in flight, we glided down and touched the water. We disembarked at the Haines dock and walked into town. We checked out the ferry and found that we couldn't get a cabin the first day but were told that we could sleep on the fantail of the ferry. We decided to go to a delicatessen and buy an assortment of cheeses, crackers, wine, beer, potato chips and fruit to last a day or two. Once aboard, we acquired two cots on the far end of the ferry. It was a lovely, sunshiny afternoon, and we relaxed as the ferry departed and the mountains passed us by. The fresh air was exhilarating. Around dinnertime, the sun began to set behind the islands. We broke out the beer, wine, and food and enjoyed the swooshing of the waves against the side of the ship. We were as completely relaxed as if we were on a cruise ship. Several hippie kids began settling in nearby, with their marijuana, beer, and wine. As darkness approached, the temperature dropped to 60 degrees, but the gas lamps warmed us. We also had ample blankets that kept us warm throughout the night. The next day, we were able to get a cabin for the remainder of the trip.

We were pretty tired from all the traveling, as the ship pulled into Sitka early in the morning. A tour group was forming to go ashore to visit a Russian church and museum. Unfortunately, we declined to go. Years later, we often wondered why we passed on the opportunity to see the town and learn about its history. The next morning, the ferry crept out through the island passageway and into the Pacific Ocean. We were awakened early by the movement of the ferry between the ocean swells and went to the cafeteria for breakfast. Later that day, the ferry arrived in Seattle. It was great to be greeted by our children and Jill's parents. Washington looked beautiful, as did our Priest Point home!

Chapter 20

Building a Nuclear-Power Plant

AFTER RETURNING FROM ALASKA, I attended a National Safety Society conference in Seattle, where I met the manager of Safety and Security for construction of the Hanford II atomic plant in Richland, WA. He was interested in my experience at Washington Natural Gas and on construction of the Alaska pipeline. He said he was moving to the corporate headquarters of Brown and Root Construction and needed someone to replace him at Hanford. Brown and Root managed 14 companies working on the nuclear-power plant project at Hanford. I would be responsible for both safety and security for the project and have authority over 14 guards, three nurses, and a safety assistant. The 14 subcontractors had a total of 1,400 construction workers.

I took the job and began the trek across the state in my 1968 Ford truck, pulling our 16-foot travel trailer. That evening, I encountered high winds and rain. The trailer was weaving back and forth from the strong crosswinds. I finally arrived in Richland and, the next morning, drove 18 miles out to the construction site. I met my boss and the construction manager, my secretary and assistant, the nurses, and security personnel. At lunch time, I became acquainted with a young engineer. His father owned a trailer park that sat along the edge of the Columbia River. Someone had vacated the best view on top of the hillside. That evening, I drove there and established myself. Conveniently, the laundry room and showers were next to my trailer, and I had an unobstructed view south, toward the Columbia River. At work the next day, I met another engineer who commuted back and forth to the Seattle area, so we decided to take turns driving home on weekends.

Measuring chemical residue.

My security responsibilities involved working with federal agents. We noticed several footprints outside the security fences surrounding the construction site. We stayed up all night for a week watching for the intruders, but whoever they were, they didn't appear.

There were times when I would have to climb down into large, galvanized tanks to read the oxygen meters. Luckily, there was never any leftover contamination, or I wouldn't have survived. I made many inspections of the 14 companies and drove my company truck down the four miles to the Columbia River and back. The most memorable event of my assignment was the day we used four giant cranes to move the main nuclear reactor into place. Three out of the four nuclear power plants were cancelled because of labor problems. The Washington Public Power Supply went bankrupt and the public shareholders lost everything that they had invested.

After a while, I brought Jill and the children over to Richland to find housing for our family. We looked around the Richland, Pasco, Kennewick area, but the wind and dust wasn't suited to us, so we never moved. Primarily because of the lack of cooperation from the unions, I decided to resign and return to the Puget Sound.

Chapter 21

High Technology and Aerospace

IN 1978, I ACCEPTED A JOB at the Eldec Corporation (now Crane) in Lynnwood, WA. The company made high tech controls for the military and NASA. My job was to coordinate technical training and management development for two divisions and career-development programs for the employees. I also assisted with the machine-shop apprenticeship program. I was appointed to the Edmonds Community College advisory council and assisted in setting up the high-tech curriculum for entry-level students.

In my training director's office.

Marjory Miller was responsible for the Circuit-Board Assembly section. Every year, I would send her to California to be recertified in the latest technologies. The company also was involved in building components for the space-shuttle program. After two years as training coordinator I was promoted to training manager. Unfortunately, I did not get the support from my boss, John Vicklund, for the budget needed to accomplish all of the training requirements that I requested.

Chapter 22

Building Computer Tutorials

IN THE EARLY 1980S, I WAS contacted by an associate from The American Society for Training and Development to join a software-development project in Kirkland. The entire group of us were professional training managers or specialists or managers who had been laid off, due to budget cuts. The project was funded by the Amway Corporation. It was the inception of the personal-computer era, but most of us didn't even own a computer. Three of us drove to Portland and bought the first IBM computers. Our office was located on the top floor of a house, near the I-405 freeway. It was a 25-mile commute from my home in Marysville. We were developing a format to project moving cartoon characters across the screen to reinforce learning concepts, but we really were not programmers. We simply followed the project manager's instructions in formatting the information needed to code and develop the tutorials. We were well paid for our work and received our checks regularly, once a month. Then suddenly, after the sixth month, no one received his monthly check. The following month, no one had been paid. Later on, some members filed a lawsuit, but I never heard if they won it. It was difficult for me, because we hadn't prepaid our quarterly income taxes. Unfortunately, I could not pay them and the Federal Department of Revenue put a lien on our house and checking accounts. We were experiencing extreme financial difficulties, having also been sued by the Tulalip

Indian tribe for an accident on Marine Drive that totaled our car. I needed to get away and find some peace of mind, so I combined a deer-hunting trip with apple-picking work in Eastern Washington. Picking apples for a couple of weeks and mixing with the migrant workers turned out to be a good experience. I also shot a buck that put some meat on our table, which made me feel much better. It was at that point that I decided to take an offer from Aramco and fly to Saudi Arabia.

Dressed in Arab garb and holding a hubbly bubbly on our camping trip in Saudia Arabia.

Chapter 23

Aramco—Saudi Arabia

AFTER I APPLIED FOR A POSITION in Saudi Arabia, I was flown to San Francisco to be interviewed. I accepted a position as an instructional designer in Dhahran. The company that hired me developed training programs for Aramco. Everything was paid—my flight to Saudi Arabia, food and lodging, and a very good salary. I was informed that a person would meet me at the airport in Washington, D.C., with a package of important information that I was to take with me to Dhahran. Unfortunately, in order to do this, I had to make two separate airport stops. I left Seattle early in the morning, after being dropped off by Jill, Kristie, and Kurt, flew to St. Paul/Minneapolis, and on to Washington D.C., then up to New York. I boarded a 747 flight that was jam-packed and took 14 hours to reach Saudi Arabia.

It was pitch black when I walked down the steps to the terminal in Dhahran. Armed guards were holding AK-47s. I had quite a few bags, and I waited in line to receive them, then showed my passport and box of information to Customs and was lead to the taxi-pickup area. A driver was parked there and he immediately introduced himself and loaded my luggage into the car. We drove in the dark to the construction camp's double-occupancy section, which had a common bathroom between two bedrooms. The next morning, I met my neighbor in the hallway and introduced myself. He was a lot younger—in his 20s maybe—and somewhat shabby looking, with not much to say except that he was a draftsman. My first impression was that he probably was a druggie.

The following morning, I was awakened by the Arab prayers emanating from loud-speakers outside. I showered and got ready for my first day of work. I was escorted to the camp cafeteria. I was very tired after traveling 28 hours and making three airplane changes. The cafeteria tables were about 14 feet long. The occupants were from all different countries, but most of them spoke English. It was fun listening to who they were, what projects they were assigned, their family backgrounds, and the different cultures they represented.

After breakfast, I was driven four miles to meet my supervisor in charge of writing training programs for Aramco's Security personnel. I had been hired as an instructional-system developer. We followed a matrix of training requirements. Every skill had to be broken down into tasks and knowledge according to the learning objectives. Personal computers still were in their infant stages, so we used typewriters to prepare the training instructions. It was fun talking to Aramco Security workers about their jobs and families. Most of them were down-to-earth individuals and lots of them had worked at U.S. military bases.

I had arrived in Saudi Arabia a few days before Thanksgiving and finally recovered from jet lag. All of a sudden. I realized that I hadn't called Jill since arriving. She and the kids were very relieved that I had arrived safely. We agreed that she would call me once a week. Because personal computers and cellphones were not yet in use, we sent cassette tapes and pictures through the mail every week. I was half a world away, and Jill was working for the Marysville-Pilchuck High School as a secretary in the athletic department and was raising our 17-year-old son and 18-year-old daughter by herself. Thankfully, we lived on Puget Sound in a quiet neighborhood, with wonderful neighbors. And Duke was there to comfort Jill, too. After the first of the year, Jill had a call to return to the Payroll Department at the Everett Boeing plant, which she said would never happen after being laid off several years before, but the good salary was very tempting.

Back in Saudi Arabia, our work group had a Christmas dinner at our supervisor's house. Even though Aramco was Arab company, they still respected us for our beliefs. Two or three days a week, four to six of us would take a bus to Bahrain and have dinner. After eating, I always went to the kitchen and thanked the chef for a fine meal. Most of the meals were Middle Eastern and deliciously spiced.

The camp complex had tennis courts, a swimming pool, and a library. After work, I would change into my bathing suit and swim several hundred laps. I met and became friends with lots of people at the pool. After swimming, I would go the library and read books and magazines. There were several TVs, which helped us to relax. There also was a snack bar, where we could buy pop and non-alcoholic beer. I'd then go back to my room, shower, and talk into my cassette recorder. Once a week, I'd mail the tapes and pictures that I had taken to Jill and the kids. And I always looked forward to receiving their tapes from home.

On weekends, my friends and I would drive to small towns far out in the desert. Along the way, we would spot wild camels and herds of sheep and goats. In the small villages, we saw goats running loose on the streets. After two hours of driving, we arrived in the town of Elkhabar. The marketplace offered a large variety of spices, clothing, colored blankets, and jewelry. Each merchant's display was in a 20x20-foot enclosure. I bought a gold necklace and pair of earrings for Jill. In a below-street-level market, I found an antique Bedouin copper coffeepot that had spent years in the desert. Down the street, we saw 20 camels, brought there to be auctioned to meat processors or for transportation on desert trips. Two boys had signs reading "Camel-Riding Pictures." After I paid for my picture, the boys placed a large pillow on the rear of a camel. They had a muzzle over the camel's mouth, and its legs were tied together. The camel I was on was mean and angry. He pulled against the rope and tried to bite my leg, all the time making loud wailing sounds. The boys held tightly onto the ropes that held the nasty beasts.

Another adventure three of us planned was a 300-mile trip to Northern Saudi Arabia to camp out in the desert. After driving past old fortresses, we arrived at a large refinery on the coast of the Arabian Sea. The water was crystal clear, and it was a beautiful, sunshiny day. A few fishermen cast their lures out into the waves. Soon, we left the two-lane highway and followed an old road across the desert. I was riding in the backseat of the jeep, when I saw a shepherd with a flock of about 50 sheep. One of my companion said, "It's like a scene right out of the Bible!" Luckily, I had my camera and caught the whole picture. Toward evening, a 20-mile-an-hour wind began blowing. We needed a place to build our campfire and cook our supper. We found a depression below some rocks, out of the wind.

Right away, my two friends donned their Arab robes and tunics. I didn't have any desert attire, only blue jeans and a sweatshirt. One friend got out his four-foot-long "hubbly bubbly" smoking apparatus and set it up next to the fire. He then broke out some homemade red wine and we all began to feeling good! We were singing songs and dancing around the campfire, when Bill tripped and fell onto the fire. We pulled him up and out quickly so he wasn't burned. His Arab camel robe was so thick that it was bareley scorched. After dark, off in the distance, we observed headlight about a half-mile from us. Then two other beaming lights appeared in the opposite direction. We quickly bedded down in our sleeping bags and fell asleep. Early the next morning, we were awakened by the sounds of camels making their high-pitched squeaks, followed by a series of female utterings. We were surrounded by three Bedouin camps. Each camp appeared to have a herd of camels. We quickly got up and walked down toward the Bedouin campsites, listening to all of the female chatter. The women were giving the camels the water that had arrived the evening before. The lights we had seen were water-tank trucks arriving in their camp. We sat on some rocks, and the camels walked out of the camp, right toward us. They walked right by my friend in Arabic garb, thinking that he was part of the normal scene. Then, they stopped and walked up to me in my jeans and sweatshirt. Their expressions were like, "What's that guy with the funny clothes doing here?" It was another beautiful, sunshiny day, with blue skies and white, puffy clouds. We were lucky, because the monthly trading activity was going on. All types of live animals were there—goats, sheep, chickens, geese, rabbits, camels, horses, dogs, and cows. There also were all types of vegetables, spices, and tools, as well as cloth and blankets. Many items were traded by Bedouins and town folks. The town itself was small, with the business buildings located on two streets. One of my companions had been a college professor, and he spoke fluent Arabic. Outside a clothing store, he struck up a conservation with the owner, who spoke English. Soon, we all became very friendly with our new acquaintance, so he invited us to come to his home for lunch. We entered his home and were seated on cushions on the floor. We continued our conversations for a while, when his wife entered the room with coffee, dates, and crackers. He did not introduce us to his wife. She returned later with our lunch and never spoke a word. We were aware that this was their culture. Afterward, we drove the 300 miles back to Bahrain, arriving later that night.

One afternoon after work, as I approached the door to my room, a helicopter pilot who lived across the hallway stopped me and said that the young man (who shared the bathroom in the duplex) was found murdered in his bed. Several Saudi police investigators were inside the murdered man's room. My first thought was I was glad that I never had touched the handle of the door to the victim's room. It appeared he never had slept there, and I hadn't seen or heard him for several months. I then went to a retired sheriff I knew, who also worked for the company. He suggested that I document what I did before, during, and after the murder. That evening, and for the following month, a Saudi guard sat all night outside my door in the hallway. I presumed that it was to protect me, and everything seemed to be going fine for about a week. I was then asked to talk to the Saudi police captain in Dhahran. He asked if I'd heard anything the night of the murder. I said I didn't and answered all of his other questions. Everything was quiet for a month, when I was asked to go in for further questioning. The captain asked the same questions again. When I said that I already answered those questions, he suddenly became angry. I was taken to a small room, where I sat for an hour. Then, two policemen took me to a dungeon-type cell in the basement. I asked how long I would be there. They said probably 20 minutes. There was a hole in the floor for a toilet. Four or five Saudi men were sitting on the floor. I waited about 35 minutes and no one came to let me out. I got upset and asked why they were still keeping me. About an hour and a half later, a Saudi guard opened the cell and took me back to the same waiting room. I stayed there again for another hour and a half, when a clean-cut Saudi man in a white robe and flat hat came in and introduced himself. He was the Saudi counterpart owner of the company that I worked for. I didn't know at the time that he had taken responsibility for me and that I needn't be placed in jail. Because it was difficult to pin guilt on anyone, they had used me as a person of interest. The Saudi was in a humorous mood and tried to calm me down.

The following day, I was driven to the U.S. State Department Embassy. I was introduced to a young United States representative and a Saudi representative who worked there. I was fortunate in that I had brought a letter with me to Saudi Arabia, signed by my congressman. The letter stated that if I ever needed assistance, he would be there to help in any way. They had read my summary of what had transpired and didn't like my treatment by the Saudi police captain. The State Department suggested that I be moved to Elkhabar, 20 miles across the bay from Dhahran, and the corporate office of my employer. The last morning at my old location, I decided I wanted to look professional, so I wore a light-blue suit and tie to the new office. After an hour, I was told to go to my hotel. Arriving there, I was greeted by the Saudi captain, who said, "Good morning, Jack." He was very cordial and friendly. I'm sure the State Department had something to do with his new attitude. I then went to my new location, where I worked for the remainder of my stay.

Me in shepherd's robe at an old fort on the Arabian Sea.

I didn't want to alarm Jill about all of the difficulties I had encountered until later. After about three weeks, I called her and explained the situation. Unfortunately, my salary had been reduced and I had to sign a letter that my company was not to blame for anything that had happened. During the first month, I had lunch with various training managers and others. I also met the secretary, who was from India, and two Saudi men, who I really liked. I was given various assignments setting up training programs.

The hotel where I stayed had about 200 rooms, a large restaurant, an Olympic-size swimming pool, and a pool parlor. I quickly made friends from all over the world. Every evening after dinner, a group—mostly from England—had a lot of fun playing pool. I especially enjoyed the English jargon for terms like, "Balls up," meaning, "Better get with it." A much larger hotel, owned by the same company, was a block away. We sometimes would go there to play snooker pool. The entrance and lobby had marble floors and columns, with high ceilings. Large, jaded-glass light fixtures were all around. It always was fun to see the mostly female flight attendants from airlines all around the world. Needless to say, there were some very beautiful ladies. Outside, there was a huge, kidney-shaped swimming pool. My office was just a couple of blocks away, so I would come for my lunch break and swim and lie in the sun. Usually, two or three of my friends would join me there.

My typical day always began by getting out of bed, putting on my bathing suit, opening my window, stepping out to the pool, and swimming laps for about 20 minutes. Afterward, I would walk a block, stop at a small grocery store, buy a box of cold cereal and milk, get to work, go to the television-production studio, have my cereal and coffee, and go about my various duties. Sometimes, I had little or nothing to do, so I would help the TV-production guys. I took up my free time developing a bowling game that I had been working on. Other times during lunch break, I would walk to the business district of Elkabar and have chicken curry or go to an ice-cream shop and get a cantaloupe shake. I don't know what was in them, but I got really "high" afterward. After a while, I began having supper at the mobile van outside the hotel, featuring goat, sheep, or camel burgers. For dessert, I would get a chocolate-dipped ice-cream cone. I'd then take a two-mile walk by the ocean to watch the sunset, then head for my room and tape letters to Jill and the kids, watch TV, and go to sleep. Once in a while, I would order pizza and eat it in my room. Weekends were spent mostly sitting around the pool, drinking non-alcoholic beer, and munching warm meats. Sometimes, my friends from the Dhahran camp would come and visit me. It was hard being away from the family. I really missed them and enjoyed talking to them once a week.

Several months later, I was informed that the police had identified the killer of the young man who lived in my duplex, and I was no longer a person of interest. In the meantime, Sim Wilson, our neighbor in Marysville and a state representative, helped me to get back to the U. S. After nine months, I was happy the day that I boarded a Jordanian jet at the airport! I said goodbye to my two production friends who had driven me to the airport. I flew over the desert and changed planes in Jordan. I then flew into an isolated landing field that sat next to the Danube River in Austria and was situated in a beautiful, green valley. There, I boarded a 747 for the flight to New York, where I changed to another plane that took me into Sea-Tac Airport. It was wonderful to embrace my family and be home again!

Chapter 24

Plumbing Business

After returning from Saudi Arabia, I found myself without a job. By this time, I was entering my 60s. Because of my age, I had trouble competing with younger applicants. My father had mentioned several times that it was always good to have a trade to fall back on. I hadn't worked in the plumbing trade for 42 years. Therefore, I needed to get credit for four years of active work experience, plus pass the Uniform Plumbing Code qualification test. The test had two main parts: water and venting. I obtained copies of the Uniform Plumbing Code and studied it. I also obtained information from Jill's former classmate, Larry Adams, a union master plumber. Three in the Fritz family were master plumbers and all practiced in South Haven: my grandfather William Adolph Fritz, my father Harry Fritz, and my brother Tom Fritz. And my cousin, Dennis Fritz, owned the William Fritz and Sons Plumbing business in South Haven. My cousin verified that I had the equivalent of four years of experience working for my father's business.

I passed the test and obtained a journeyman's plumbing license. In order to get some on-the-job familiarization, I flew back to Kalamazoo, MI, and worked for my brother, Tom. This helped quite a lot, but I still needed more on-the-job experience. After returning to the Northwest, I worked for several plumbing contractors. Most of them hired young, on-the-job trainees, who were called "Tennis

Shoe Plumber's Helpers." In the 1980s, large contractors were building huge complexes of homes, most of them the same style. These younger boys were literally running up and down stairs, piecing together the water and drain pipes. This was the time when plumbing piping had just changed from metal to composite plastic, which was much faster to install.

I also found that the plumbing culture had changed. Many plumbing-business owners were on drugs. On one occasion, I had just nailed the wooden backing for attaching a lavatory. The owner, a six-foot-two, 250 pound man, took his hammer and demolished my wooden backing, then fired me. After working for other owners with similar attitudes, I decided to start my own business. It was called Priest Point Plumbing.

My first job was doing the plumbing for a trailer park on the Tulalip Indian Reservation. Shortly after that, the tribe obtained a grant to train 10 young members as potential plumbers. I would demonstrate soldering and other installation techniques. Most of them were hesitant to do the "hands-on" training. During the first year in my business, I was fortunate that it was an extremely cold Winter and there were frozen pipes everywhere. It kept me very busy! Lots of plumbers directed work to me, but it was "grunt work" that they didn't want to do—like busting up concrete on repair work. After two years in business, I was not doing that great. It proved to be stressful, so I began working temporarily for a construction-placement company.

Chapter 25

Interim Jobs (Contract work)

WHEN I WAS IN-BETWEEN REGULAR WORK, my friend, Dale Laurin, would hire me to do special assignments for NovaTech Engineering, with offices in Seattle and Lynnwood. My first job was writing federal-grant applications. I would determine whether the company could qualify to compete, with the objectives outlined in the proposal. I then would talk to the engineers about how, when, and at what cost the work could be accomplished. These engineers were the "content-methods experts." I wrote what objectives we could accomplish, the cost, the approach, and the schedule for the project to be completed. My experience as project director of the grant for the centralized training facility at Fort Casey State Park for the Washington State Park Department was useful here. I also made use of my mathematics background in estimating the cost of irregular-shaped concrete structures. And I updated the NovaTech standards library.

My most fun assignment was writing and putting together an owner/operating manual for Rago Wagner, a heavy-equipment manufacturer. NovaTech had obtained a contract to build a Strad-80 container loader for them. It would be similar to those that load and unload container ships throughout the world. But it was unique in that the hoists were diesel-powered and the wheels were powered by electricity. All four wheels could move 360 degrees, enabling them to operate in tight lanes on the waterfront. I talked to Dale Laurin about the assignment and told him that I'd never done technical writing." He said, "You can do it, Jack!" He also mentioned that the operating manual needed to be completed in a month, and that the first production vehicle was being tested at the Seattle waterfront.

The next day, I flew to Portland and became familiar with Rago Wagner operating manuals that were written primarily for the logging industry. First thing next morning, I drove to the Seattle waterfront, climbed into the cab next to the loader operator, and noted the steps he took to maneuver over the containers, grasp them, and move them to the large cranes that hoisted the containers onto the ships. I then took pictures of all of the controls inside the cab. Every day, I obtained information from mechanical and electrical engineers on how the vehicle functioned and what maintenance requirements needed to be accomplished. I broke down the different functions in chapters, inserted pictures, and sent the information to a publisher. Needless to say, it took nearly two months before the manual was completed.

Because of my experience as an employment manager for Western Gear, I next was hired by the Lynnwood Equipment Company to work in job placement. They sold heavy equipment to the construction and logging industries. The first couple of months, I hired operators and was paid a commission for it. Whenever these operators quit or were fired, my commission would cease. Of course, in the construction industry, this happens all the time. Pretty soon, I realized that I was being taken advantage of and I quit.

Another enjoyable job I picked up during some of my down time was as a longshoreman in Everett, unloading logs that arrived on the waterfront. From our house at Priest Point, I would watch for log container ships coming in, and I would rush down to the longshore office and sign up to unload the logs. It was a good-paying job.

Chapter 26

Apartment Ownership

Jill's father, Chester Johnson, built the Talbot Road Apartments all by himself, after retiring from the Seattle Police Department. He was the type of guy who couldn't sit around and be bored. He designed plans for a nine-unit, three-story apartment building, after visiting other apartment buildings in the area. His plans were accepted at the Snohomish County Building Department in Everett, and he was given a permit to build. The City of Edmonds was about to annex the property, so he had to hurry to pour the footings for the foundation. I was dating Jill in 1963 and helped spread the concrete for the first of the three floors. From that point on, Chet did everything—the framing, the brickwork, the electrical, the plumbing, the sheetrock, the cupboards, and the roof. What he didn't know, he took a class or read up on how to do it. It took him about 17 years to finish the building, but then he didn't always work long days at it. Since they lived just down the hill from the apartment building and it was a nice day, he would quit early, invite neighbors, and enjoy his 20x40-foot, saltwater swimming pool. He was very talented, but he always was looking for a certain tool that he had mislaid somewhere. Jill's mom finally got a school secretary job after she claimed she spent too much time looking for Chet's tools! But she did spend her weekends helping clean and reorganize them.

Doris and Chet Johnson (Jill's parents).

    Jill's dad was so handy that he did all the preventative maintenance and upkeep himself. He kept all the apartments rented and had a "waiting list," because he charged the very minimum rent. He believed he would have to pay more income tax if he charged more. In 1998, when he was 90, he began talking about selling the apartment building. Considering that he charged low rents, we thought that he might sell the property below what apartments were selling for at the time. I asked Jill if maybe we should buy the apartment building to help with our own retirement. We asked her parents what they thought about the idea, and were surprised how willingly they would accept the idea. Our payments were to be $1,000 a month for the rest of their lives. We also would be required to pay the taxes, the utility bills, and any maintenance costs. We were able to raise the rents without any objection from her parents. We drafted a letter to all the tenants saying that the rent would be increased by $25 a month, from the $325 they were paying. Not one occupant moved out. (Incidently, now in Seattle a studio apartment is renting from $1,500 to $2,000 a month). Now, in the Summer of 2020, we are renting our apartments for $1,400 a month.

I find this little line from poet, T.S. Eliot, to be appropriate: *"Only those who will risk going too far can possibly find out how far one can go."*

But in order for us to eventually take over the title to the apartment building, the one acre had to be subdivided into three parcels. Unfortunately, after scheduling a hearing for short platting the family property, the City Council postponed the hearing indefinitely. It took eight years and many more dollars to finally get the short plat approved. The main reason for the delay is that the mayor of the city didn't like the idea of infilling. In the meantime, we had rented out our Priest Point home and moved into the penthouse of the apartment and were the property managers. Since we had to downsize from a big, three-story house to a one-bedroom penthouse, most of our furniture went to our son, Kurt, and his new bride. Our daughter was off on her own by then, so we were empty nesters. We both were working at Boeing, so the drive to the Everett plant actually was a little shorter, and we soon adjusted to the smaller residence and learned to love it. We ended up living there for 20 years and were there to help Jill's parents during their last years. In 2010, Jill's dad, who lived to be 102, and her mother 94, both passed away within four months of each other, still living in their original home that Chet built in 1945.

Occasionally, there were emergencies in the apartment. One day in 1999, I needed some help replacing a leaky hot-water heater. I noticed a young man working just down the street and he came to my aid. His name was Milynn Wetzel, and he was a journeyman carpenter, plumber, electrician, and welder. He was a healthy, good-looking young man, who could have been a model or movie star. Milynn was raised on a farm in North Dakota, a good place to learn a lot about how to fix farm equipment and also how to form a good work ethic. In 2000, Jill and I became snowbirds, driving to Arizona in the Winter, but we never had to worry. When we had an emergency, Milynn was there to handle it. After returning from Arizona, I would find preventive-maintenance projects for him to work on. Milynn and I became good friends, and I would help him on the grunt work. He would come in the evening, and we would work together, often splitting a six pack of Blue Moon beer. We replaced hot water heaters, remodeled bathrooms, fabricated metal railings, updated ventilating fans, and lots of other jobs. It was more like fun than work. We could find humor in almost any topic. Over the years, I have taken Milynn as my godson. He has always been there whenever I have needed him. I'll always cherish his companionship.

The apartment building has given us great pleasure! It gives me something to keep myself occupied and creative, especially in the Summer months when we are in Washington. Without the income from it, we probably could not have retired so early and been able to enjoy the Winters in Arizona and the Summers in Washington.

Priest Point home.

Shortly after Chet and Doris passed away, our Priest Point home became available, after renting it out for 20 years, so we decided to move back into it, make updates, and eventually sell it. We started out with only the furniture from the penthouse, which only filled the living room, so we eventually had to buy more of everything. We painted the whole house before moving back and had carpet installed over the oak wood floors, which is just the opposite of what people were doing in new homes in 2020. After a couple of years, we remodeled the master bath and the kitchen but left the oak cabinets, which still were beautiful.

Puget Sound view from our front porch.

We return from Arizona every year at the end of April. When I get up in the morning, I go to the kitchen and light the gas fireplace, fix coffee, retrieve the morning paper, and sit down by the fireplace and read the paper. During the day, I work outside or return from our apartment projects and take a refreshing shower. Then it's out to the front porch to enjoy the sweeping views: Mount Rainier, the Naval base, Jetty Island with kite surfers jumping through the waves, ships moving into Everett, yachts and sailboats, the Mukilteo ferries, the lighthouse at Mukilteo, the three islands—Camano, Hat, and

Whidbey, the Cascade Mountains and the trains going both directions across the bay. Seagulls and eagles soar by, and the hummingbirds greet us before drinking from our "hotlips" plant. The freshness of the salt air fills our lungs, as we watch the whales spouting in Port Gardner Bay. The flowered shrubs and trees enclose us in a canopy of green and multi-colored plants. The water in Port Gardner Bay changes from calm to crested white caps when the wind changes. Above the water, the clouds take different shapes and colors. It's the ideal location to indulge in cocktails, snacks, and a leisurely dinner. The property has given us so much pleasure the last 54 years, both in lifestyle and rental income. When the weather begins turning colder, usually the first part of October, we're ready to head south, following the migrating geese.

In front of my beloved Swedish fireplace.

Chapter 27

Combination-Spares Bowling (My Invention)

IT SEEMS THAT IN THE EARLY MORNING the brain can, focus more clearly and objectively. It has a way of solving situations and creating new concepts and ideas. One such morning, I laid in bed and thought about a 10-pin, spares bowling game. I had only bowled a few times, so why would I be thinking of a new way of someone improving their play? The idea occurred to me that it wasn't the strikes that were most important, because the majority of play involved spares. I envisioned that if a spares-setting machine could be invented, then a player could practice or play spares games to improve their skills. I thought about various spares pin placements, some easier and some ever more difficult. I decided after a while that I would develop a game called Combination Spares Bowling. I went to the local library and checked out a book that depicted the steps in developing a game. The first step was to define the characteristics of the game. Then, you had to develop the rules by which the game is played. The basic concept was that a player had 10 rolls at various combinations of pin settings. The settings with the greatest degree of difficulty would receive the highest point values. The values of each successful roll then are added up to determine the final score.

    I decided to have three modes of play. The first would be a single-pin setting for every roll. The second would be a mix of different spares combinations. The third mode was based on the total number of pins knocked down. I then designed a score sheet showing the designated pin locations for each mode. The next step was to contact a patent and copyright attorney in Seattle. They completed the copyright application and sent it to Washington, D.C. At this point, I was ready to market the game. I contacted Paul Gaston, who was chief counsel for Brunswick Corporation, and he set up a meeting for me in Chicago At that time, I couldn't afford to go to Chicago and didn't go, knowing that they probably wouldn't give me what I needed anyway. And I didn't want to sit in front of a number of corporate lawyers.

All this time, I had no idea what a non-disclosure agreement was. I went to a company in Denver that overhauls pin-setting machines and develops new ones. I met with the president and his engineers and explained the concept. I returned to Washington and they never contacted me, and I couldn't reach their president. What they were doing, in partnership with Brunswick, was using my ideas to build their own games. They used them for their own bowling companies first and then brought them to bowling-alley owners. The greatest potential for the game is in gambling. Right now, the local Angel of the Winds casino is using AMF pin-setting machines for Strick, a game developed in Italy that is similar to mine. I've thought of licensing the game to Indian tribes, and I believe my grandson, Hunter, could carry the idea forward. I've learned some lessons of what not to do and could help him to get started. Hopefully, he can become a multimillionaire!

Me with children of the Serengeti families.

Chapter 28

Travels and Trips

SINCE WE RETIRED, WE HAVE SKIED many different areas in the country—Vail, Steamboat Springs, Taos, Telluride—and taken several different ski trips to Europe—but we've always loved Sun Valley the most.

While still working at Boeing, we traveled to Meyerhofen, Austria, with the Boeing Ski Club. What a great adventure that was. There were miles and miles of ski lifts and runs up and down the valley. We stayed in a chalet-style pension that raised their own calves. There probably were 200 people from many different countries. The live music and dancing at night was spectacular. We became very good friends with Mike and Carol Myers, who had just retired from Boeing and had recently moved to Semiahmoo, near the Canadian border, after living on a houseboat. We all have since then bought German attire and attended an Oktoberfest somewhere almost every year—mainly in Leavenworth, WA, or Mt. Angel, OR. We lost Carol a couple of years ago but still get together with Mike, who always plans the next year's trip. Mike is very fluent in German, so he likes to practice with other German-speaking Oktoberfest participants.

Since we began going to Arizona in the Winter, we have gotten to know "Dan, the Skiman," who runs Morningside Ski trips out of Tucson. We have been on several of his great trips, each lasting two weeks at a different resort. The last trip we were on with his group was to Zermatt, Switzerland, where he had arranged for all of us to ski down a glacier. We all were harnessed, in case we got to close to one of the many crevasses. It was quite an experience. He also would arrange dinner parties in private homes in the Alps. We had to give him a bad time once when we were served "mac and cheese," after he had arranged for cheese fondue! And we got to ski down with torches at night. It was beautiful to see the long line of fire going down the mountain.

Oktoberfest dancing in Blaine, WA.

On one of the trips in France, a group of us left Chamonix and made plans to have lunch in a small village in Italy, on the border of France. We all skied in a "follow the leader" line, with me bringing up the rear. But somehow, I didn't see them turn in a different direction, so I continued skiing on my own, thinking I could find them and meet them for lunch. But I ended up in another village in Italy! France, Italy, and Switzerland all border each other right in that area. I finally realized that I'd gotten detached from my group, after waiting quite a while for them to arrive. I decided I'd better head back to Chamonix, and I ended up taking several different lifts, all going in different locations. I didn't get back to our pension until dark. The group was getting ready to send out a search party for me, especially Jill, who was very worried! It was quite an adventurous day.

Reconnecting with Navy buddy, Shelly ("Ski") Schwab in Idaho.

Dan is a retired school teacher and worked for a travel agency in the Summer months, so he knows how to organize the whole trip for a good price, which can include a side trip, either before or after the two weeks. Once, we spent an entire week in Paris in a hotel that our daughter paid for with some of her hotel points. We also took side trips to Prague and Amsterdam. And Dan always had a comfortable bus for us to get around, even on little weekend skiing trips near Arizona.

We still enjoy skiing and especially like the Sunrise Ski Resort in the White Mountains of southeast Arizona, near Show Low. It's operated by the Apache Indians, and the many runs are very challenging. It's not that far for us to travel for a three- or four-day outing. At the time, we had a van that we used to love. We would park it at the ski area, have cocktails, cook our dinner, and watch the wild animals that would come out at night. We parked the van in many wonderful spots over the years. One was in the Mt. St. Helen's area, after it erupted, overlooking Spirit Lake, where Harry Truman's remains are interred. He used to own the Mt. St. Helens Lodge, before the mountain blew it all away. When Jill and I were first married, we were up hunting in that area, when a snowstorm forced us into his lodge for the night. It was quite an experience, as it was just us, Harry, another friend, and a million cats in the lodge, with no power. He showed us to an upstairs room that had no lock on the door, but we wedged a chair against the door for security. We knew Harry didn't like hunters. Luckily, we had taken off our red hunting clothes, because they were soaking wet—and put on other clothes! Another time in the van, we went to Coupeville on Whidbey Island for New Year's Eve, parking in front of Toby's Tavern. It was snowing very hard, so after closing down the place, we walked maybe 10 feet to our van and curled up for a good night's sleep!

Not long before retiring from Boeing, we planned a two-week rafting trip on the Colorado River. That trip is the one that really got us hooked on Arizona. We had no idea there were so many beautiful mountains throughout the state. We arrived in Flagstaff with our proper river gear, clothing, sleeping bags, and lots of beer to meet up with the 16 other rafters. The next morning, they bused us to Lee's Ferry, where we started our 10-day rafting trip. We would exit just before Lake Mead. Besides the vacationers, we were accompanied by the captain of the raft, a photographer, and a college geology student who was narrating the whole trip. Tents were provided for us at night, and all the food was beautifully prepared. The 20-foot-long by eight-foot-wide rubber raft was motorized and sat quite high on the water, with a lot of storage below for all of the gear. After breakfast, the gear would be loaded chain-style, and we would hop aboard and drift or motor over the surging river. Near lunchtime, we would pull up onto a sandy beach. After lunch, we would hike up into the small canyons and swim in warm ponds. It was a wonderful vacation!

We've taken several cruises over the years, the first to the eastern Caribbean in 1992. We went with a group of Jill's high school friends—20 in all—on the Star Princess. We left from Puerto Rico and traveled more than 1,200 miles, hitting five ports of call. We spent an extra three days after the cruise, visiting San Juan and staying in a pension that looked as if the movie "Casablanca" was filmed there.

In the Fall of 1998, Jill and I flew to Frankfort, Germany, as the beginning of a five-week road trip around central Europe. Halfway through the flight, we pushed our seats back and dozed off. Sometime during the night, a flight attendant asked if we wanted anything. All of a sudden, I realized we had entered another time zone and it was October 5th. I said, "Wow, it's our wedding anniversary"! She said "Wait, I'll be right back Soon, she brought us a bottle of champagne and a gold Northwest Airlines winged pin. She was such a sweetheart!

Immediately after landing, we boarded a train for Munich. We had eight suitcases and duffle bags and jumped on board. The train whisked past villages and towns at breathtaking speeds. At one point, the train stopped, the doors opened, and we carried our bags quickly onto the dock, thinking that this was the location to transfer to another train. We noticed that the name of the stop was incorrect. We barely were able to gather our things and reenter the train before the doors closed. We later discovered that the bag containing our hiking shoes was missing. Four years later, the bag was returned to us in the states!

Later in the afternoon, we checked into the Munich Marriott Hotel for a week's stay, again paid for with our generous daughter's hotel points. We visited downtown Munich, first stopping at the old church, with 200 steps rising to the top of the bell tower. Directly below, we viewed the Glockenspiel's tiny figures doing their dance. We enjoyed the food and beers and other sites for two more days, and then we rented a small station wagon and drove out to Dachau. Arriving there, we were hungry for sauerbraten. At the "Drei Rofen," a small restaurant, the waitress asked, in German what we wanted to eat. We didn't see any words on the menu that looked like sauerbraten, and she couldn't understand us, as she spoke no English. After several misunderstandings, I pointed to a picture of some cows, stood up, and blurted out, "Moo, moo, moo." She finally understood! Later that day we toured the Dachau concentration camp, which was very depressing. Our sister-in-law, Inge, who is married to Jill's brother, lived in Dachau in her younger years, with her grandmother, mother, and two brothers, after her father was killed in the war. She clearly remembers, when the war was finally over, helping the survivors carry their few belongings to the waiting trains.

Afterward, we drove east into Austria. The farms were covered in red, yellow, and gold flowers, and the hillsides were green with oats and still-growing Winter wheat. We continued east along the Danube River to Krems and registered at a 400-year-old hotel, right next to the river. It's interesting to note that my uncle, Harold Fritz, was stationed near there for eight months with the U.S. Army occupational force, after the German surrender.

The following morning, we had breakfast in the courtyard. We rented bikes and waited for the barge to carry us across to the other side of the Danube River. We cycled until noon and had a beer outside an inn, watching the tour boats float by. Heading back upriver, I noticed a castle high up on a knoll and learned it was the Aggstein Castle. We stopped at a local shop, where we met a gentleman with a truck who offered to transport us and our bikes all the way up to the castle, which was on a steep, winding road. We learned that King Richard the Lionhearted of England was held there and later released, when England paid his ransom in gold to the castle inhabitants. We had lunch and beers in a reconditioned section of the castle. It was a wonderful stop and a fun bike ride back down to the river road.

The next day we drove to Waidhofen, where our sister-in-law's niece, Doris, and her family lived. The small village is situated in a valley that leads up to the mountains. The following day, we all took a hike in the Naturpark Otscher-Formauer. A series of waterfalls flowed down the creeks that drained into the river below. After hiking through beautiful farms and meadows, out of nowhere there appeared a farmer's home that was open to the public, so we stopped and had lunch.

On the road again, we headed south into northeast Italy, where we drove through a series of tunnels, some up to 10 miles long. Three hours later, we were in Venice, on the Adriatic Sea. We enjoyed the gondola rides and long walks through and around the city. Next we stayed overnight at Lucignano and the famous hilltop town of San Semegnano. It was a crisp, rainy day and I was coming down with a cold, so we bought a bottle of brandy—and that cured it! We walked all day and climbed some of the towers. Later in the afternoon, we rented a small upstairs room on the edge of town. I noticed that the sidewalk nearby was roped off for construction. After dinner and in the dark, we headed for our room, but since we hadn't written down the address, we had to wander for at least 45 minutes through the narrow, winding streets until something looked familiar. Finally, we met a lady coming out of a building and asked her if our room might be in there, and she said yes, so she let us in. The next day a full-sized pig was being roasted in the plaza, so we bought some pork for the road and drove west to the Italian Riviera.

We arrived in Riomaggiore, and we wanted a room by the water and finally met a person who took us to one we could rent for a night or two. Our room was on the fourth floor, up a narrow, winding staircase. We looked right out and down on the Mediterranean Sea. We bought wine, cold cuts, cheese, and bread from the grocer downstairs and ate outside on the little deck. What a romantic spot!

The next day, we took the train north to Monterossa, where we wanted to walk the famous trail along the Le Cinque Terre, widely promoted by Edmonds, WA-based tour guru—Rick Steves. The trail wound through vineyards, small houses, bushes, and olive trees. About five hours later, we were back at Monterossa having dinner, once again on our deck, watching the waves lapping against the walls below.

We woke to another beautiful day, and instead of backtracking 100 miles south, we decided to head straight east and find the main freeway. After driving about 30 miles north along the coast, we came to a small village. We were hungry for breakfast but found that everything was closed. While walking through the village, we met a jolly older Italian coming out of his basement, where he had been attending his wine room. "Would you like a taste?" he asked in very broken English. "Yes," we replied. He then filled two giant mugs with red wine for us. We stayed quite a while while finishing the wine and trying to communicate with him. We didn't want to leave any wine and hurt his feelings! We thanked him and staggered back to our car. That was our breakfast that day. After a short nap, we drove east on a one-lane road that was covered with branches and leaves. We felt like Christopher Columbus. On and on, round and round, up and down for two hours, in the pouring rain, we finally found the freeway.

We made it into France. We stayed overnight in Monaco, then continued west for a while, stopping to tour the towns of Abbaye de Montmajour and Annecy. We loved Annecy, with a river running through it and beautiful parks with swans, small shops, and colorful flowers. We drove north and could see Mt. Blanc in the distance. Soon, we arrived at Chamonix, where we stayed at the hotel Le Chamonix. That evening, we had fondue with small yellow potatoes, which we'd never seen before. It was a good change from bread. Next day, we took a gondola 4,000 feet up to view the mountains. We walked through spectacular ice caves on our way outside, where just walking a short distance to the top of a small hill would take our breath (and oxygen) away. It was a spectacular view, looking down on the mountain tops and glaciers, not realizing that a few years later we would be skiing down that same glacier.

We soon were off again to Switzerland. One afternoon, we came across a small village. I can't recall the name of the place, but we loved it, as it looked exactly like a chapter out of "Heidi." There were beautiful cows everywhere, with the big bells around their necks, and the sounds were tranquillizing. The hills were so green and sweet smelling. By now, we were almost to the end of October, and everything was shutting down from the tourist season. The afternoon was warm and sunny. We were looking for a place to spend the night, and someone suggested we stay at the Peter Hans Hotel. We ended up being the only guests, and it was a great place. We had a nice dinner, then we were off to bed. The next morning, the hotel employees said they'd had a big "closing-down" party and the owner felt bad he didn't let us know, as he said we would have enjoyed it. Darn! We missed out on the big celebration of dancing and drinking.

Jill and I continued our drive, winding down into the valley and into Interlaken. This road reminded us of one of the Tour de France routes. We looked up at the 1,362-foot-tall Mt. Jungfrau and the whole range of the Swiss Alps. We drove up to the village of Gruenewald and checked into a small lodge called the Hotel Alpenhof. The next morning, we caught the train for the 12,000-foot vertical climb that ended just below Mt. Jungfrau. It was a clear, sunshiny day, and we took the elevator down and hiked onto the glacier. After making our way back down the mountain, we sat down for a dinner. The owners were very cheery and were celebrating their vacation break right along with us. The following day, we began our drive up and through the mountains, heading east. We had breakfast at a small farming village. Afterward, I helped a young girl herd her cows back into the barn. I'm not sure how she would have done it alone, but I waved my hands and the cows jumped the fence and ran along the road, with me chasing them back toward the barn. It was like a wild-West roundup, without the horses! Plus, along the way, we had to stop in the road several times and wait for the livestock crossing the road. Many farmers were bringing their herds down from the upper pastures to get them ready for either the market or the barns for the Winter.

Having wine in the pension on our last night in Switzerland.

One of the last great cities we visited was Rothenburg, a hilltop town in Germany. We got a room at the Geldenen Rose Hotel and quickly joined a walking tour. One of the Japanese tourists in our group was carrying his big camera case very carefully, when the strap on the case broke. I joked with him and said, "Ha, ha—made in Japan?" He laughed back and said, "No, made in the USA!" Everyone in the group had a good laugh. It seems everywhere we went, people were so friendly and happy and the language barrier was no problem, except at the beginning of our trip in Dachau.

One morning, a few days later, we were having trouble finding the main freeway. A young man in his vehicle stopped and asked if we needed help. He explained to us where it was, but we were having trouble understanding his directions. Then, all of a sudden, he indicated he would lead us to the freeway (autobahn in German)." Once there, he stopped and pointed to the access ramp. We offered to pay him, but he said, "No, no, no." We thanked him, and he drove off.

We had to catch our plane in Frankfurt, and we arrived late at night. We returned our rental car and set out to find a hotel. Unfortunately, every hotel we tried was booked, and there also was a major strike going on with taxi drivers, police, and we didn't know who else. It was a nightmare! We finally got our luggage and ourselves into the terminal, where our plane was to leave early the next morning. We ended up spending the entire night trying to sleep on the hard seats, where we couldn't even stretch out. But we had to count our blessings, as it was the only night in five weeks that we couldn't find a room to spend the night. When our plane arrived in Seattle the next day, Jill's brother, Dave, was there to meet us and drive us home. Overall, our trip was wonderful!

We took another cruise in 2010, when we flew to Montreal, Canada, and sailed the Saint Lawrence River to Boston. We did a little family search in the library on the Silvers—Jill's side of the family. Our ship stopped for one day in Bar Harbor, ME, where our swim coach and his wife, Doug and Nancy Springer, spent their Summers. They drove us to see Arcadia National Park and other sites and then to lunch. Once we were in Boston, we spent a few extra days there. It had been our second time visiting, but there is so much to see in Boston. We loved it!

In Kenya with some native boys who were on their own for six months, entering manhood.

October of 2012 brought us a two-week safari in Tanzania and Kenya. Jill and I arrived in Kenya's capital of Nairobi. We stayed overnight in a beautiful hotel with enough scrumptious food for an army laid out for breakfast. We then left that morning on a flight to Mombasa, a resort on the Indian Ocean, where the food, service, and accommodations were excellent. The first day, we toured the town. The next morning we took a chartered boat out in the Indian Ocean, where we snorkeled and saw fish and other underwater life. We spent the afternoon on the beach, where a lot of native boys challenged me to a foot race. They all beat me very easily. I then arranged races among them, drawing a start and finish line in the sand. I lined them all up and shouted, "Go." Soon, more boys showed up, and quite a few more races took place. It was fun, seeing how excited they were. The next day, we flew back to Nairobi and were briefed by a very professional lady about our safari schedule. We put our luggage into a small bus and were driven outside the city, where we met our tour guide. We then traveled most of the day to our first of 10 different lodges that we would be staying in during the safari. All of the lodges had excellent food and accommodations. After the first five days, we changed tour guides and just two other tourists joined us, as we were then in Tanzania for the second half of our safari. October is a quiet month in Africa, as most people want to come in the wet season of November and December, when the wildebeests are migrating in the Serengeti. But we had many great days enjoying the scenes of beautiful and magnificent wildlife.

Our 50th wedding anniversary on a cruise ship in Hawaii.

Our last cruise was a week on the Norwegian Cruise Line around the Hawaiian Islands in October of 2013 to celebrate our 50th wedding anniversary. We spent the first week on the island of Kauai, hoping to see the beautiful flowers, but it was the wrong time of the year. After the cruise, we spent two nights in Honolulu and stayed in a very nice hotel, again using Kristie's points that she gave as an anniversary gift. But by the time we got checked in, it was late and we were on a high-rise floor, supposedly with an ocean view. The "boom-boom" from the band was blaring up into our room, and we couldn't even hear each other, even with the windows closed tightly. We finally got our room changed to a different side of the hotel, and it was much quieter, but we didn't have an ocean view.

Jill being kissed by a dolphin.

The next day was the most exciting. We were bused to the other side of the island and had a long-anticipated swim with the dolphins—the highlight of the whole trip. It was quite a thrill! We had a reservation the next day to tour Pearl Harbor. Unfortunately, it was shut down that day (and that day only), because our government had run out of money! So we walked the beach all day, as we had to fly home early the next day.

In 2016, our long-anticipated trip to Norway finally arrived. We looked forward to finding our ancestors' homes, after doing family searches for many years. Our great friend and SaddleBrooke neighbor, Sue Haller, who is of Norwegian descent, had helped us in setting up our trip and translating family records for us. She was a flight attendant for Flying Tiger in her younger years and eventually moved to California, after getting married. Afterward, she started her own tourist company in San Jose, CA. Unfortunately, we lost her in November of 2016, after traveling with her in Norway in May, not realizing it would be her last trip to her beloved Norway.

Prior to meeting her in Oslo for their Constitution Day on May 17, we planned a one-week trip to Ireland via Vagabond Tours. Our plane landed in Dublin fairly early in the morning. Realizing we couldn't check into our hotel until early afternoon, we opted to walk to our hotel. It turned out to be quite a hike, with our luggage and all, but at least we got a good look at how the city was laid out. We still had a couple of hours to kill after arriving at the hotel. We had a short nap, then headed into downtown for dinner. The next morning, we met our tour bus and the other 14 people we'd be spending the week with. Our guide was a local and very knowledgeable and entertaining. If he wasn't talking to us he would put on some great Irish music. We headed out of Dublin, south to Waterford, where we learned they don't make the classic Waterford crystal there anymore but now make it in Japan. We did tour another glass company near Cork, which made beautiful glasses. Our tour took us to the west coast of Dingle Bay, stopping at Killarney along the way. The last larger city was Galway, with a picturesque, seaside location. Other highlights were the Cliffs of Moher, the Blarney Castle, where we all kissed a certain rock for good luck, St. Patrick's Cathedral and several different breweries, distilleries, and quaint restaurants. Our hotels all had castle-like architecture. At the end of our tour, we returned to our original hotel and we the next two days on our own in Dublin.

We made contact with a Quigley family, who we hoped would be related to Jill's great grandfather, Martin Quigley, who was born in

Dublin in 1757. We later learned that these Quigleys were not close relatives. We really enjoyed the tour of the seven-story Guinness Brewery, built in 1759 and our free pint in the tasting room. The next day, we flew from Dublin to Trondheim, Norway, and checked into a hotel. The next morning, we went walking and saw the cathedral built in 1100 by the Vikings. We then went to a car-rental agency, picked up a car, and headed south to the town of Roros, known for its copper, discovered around 1640. It's also one of Europe's oldest preserved wooden towns. We spent a night there and drove the next day to the town of Oppdal, where we had reservations for several nights at the nearby town of Albu, where my ancestor, Ole Albu, was born. We first visited the Oppdal cemetery and found many Albu headstones. (We found Albu spelled many different ways: Aalbu, Aalbue, Albue).

Standing in front of a primitive Irish hut.

After visiting the cemetery, we drove farther up the road, trying to find the actual little town that was listed on the map. We finally spotted two workers outside their shop, so I stopped and asked them where the town of Albu was. The young man answered, "I'm an Albu!" He spoke very good English. After much talking, he called his parents, who lived just down the road, and they said they'd be happy to have us visit. We were very excited. They were so nice and also spoke very good English. They offered us coffee and some sweets and, after a while, directed us down the road to another house, where they said Ole Albue was born and raised. They called ahead for us, and we proceeded down the road to meet Knut and Heidi Aalbu, who lived in the original 300-year-old, two-story farmhouse. They were dairy farmers and had a large herd that they housed in the barn until they took them to the mountains for the Summer. The farm had many acres of grassland, but they save that for cutting in the Summer so they can feed the cattle in the Winter, as their growing season is so short. We were there mid-May, and the snow was still on the ground, but that didn't stop Knut from running around in his shorts—a real Viking! We had a great visit with them and they invited us to come back the next day when Knut's sister, Hege, who lived not far away, would come to visit with us. He said she was the real genealogist in the family and would be able to help us out.

Enjoying a Guinness beer at the Irish brewery.

The Aalbues, my ancestors from Norway.
From left, Hege, her brother, Knut, me, and Heidi, Knut's wife.

The original 300-year old Aalbue home, torn down and rebuilt after World War II.

We picked up gifts for their young children in town and headed back there the next morning. We had a wonderful visit, with more delicious sweetbreads. Their house, which had been passed down from generation to generation, was furnished with antique collectables and pictures of ancestors. Knut told us the story of how, during the Second World War, a German general arrived on a Friday night and said they would be taking over the two-story house for their troops on Monday. As soon as he left, all of the Albues in the valley got together and dismantled the log-style house, hiding the logs in the woods. When the general came on Monday morning, there was no house to be found! He didn't say if they hid from the Germans that morning, but I'm sure they did! After the war ended, the house was reassembled in its original form. It was a great visit, and we've corresponded often with our new relatives, the Aalbue's. The next day, we drove on to try to get to Oslo in time to meet Sue and two other friends from SaddleBrooke, who also were on the tour. We stopped at Lillehammer on our way south but were not very impressed. It wasn't the quaint little Norwegian city we envisioned, probably since the Olympics, held there in 1994, had commercialized it. We did spend the night and arrived at our hotel in Oslo the next morning to meet our friends.

Our Hotel Europa was a block from the Royal Palace. Since Sue was staying outside of town at her cousin Britt's house, she arranged to deliver flowers and a Norwegian flag to our room. We all met for dinner on the waterfront and planned for the next day's big celebration of the Norwegian independence day of May 27. We learned very fast how patriotic the Norwegians are! Everyone was dressed in their ethnic outfits—each district wearing a different, colorful bunad for the women and folk costume for the men. The parade in front of the palace, with the King and his family on the balcony waving, began early and ended late. We believe every school child in the city walked by, with their flags waving. The older ones held large flags straight out in front and then raised the flags, when they were directly in front of the King.

After spending several hours in the midst of the celebration, Sue gave us a whirlwind tour of Oslo, beginning at the Akershus Fortress on the waterfront. That was followed by a boat trip to the other side of the bay to the Kon Tiki and Viking Museums, a bus ride to Frogner Park, with sculptures by Gustav Vigeland, and a tram ride to the top of Ski Jump Mountain. We ended the day at Britt's apartment, with all of her family and a wonderful smorgasbord dinner, including several types of pickled herring and ending with a good shot of Aquavit.

The next day we rented a larger car for the six of us and ventured out to the small town of Saltness, where Sue spent her Summers growing up. We visited her best friend and her son, Espen, who gave us a great tour of the surrounding areas. It included the whale museum, where Espen's deceased father had spent his working life as a whaler, being gone to sea most of the year.

Finally, it was time to find where Jill's ancestors, the Johansens, lived. Their town was called Baastad, about 60 miles northeast of Oslo. Sue had arranged to have us meet, Ragnhild, a local genealogist, at the Baastad Church. She drove us to the farm where Jill's family lived, and we met Bjorn Bjornstad, who now lives in the original farmhouse. They walked with us down a long, steep hill to the edge of the lake to show us where the Johansen cottage had sat. We could see the original foundation and plot of land, where they had a garden, a cow, a pig, and chickens. Bernhardt, Jill's great grandfather, was born in that house. His father, Johan, worked on a cattle farm part-time. In exchange for his services the family was provided the small house and they were called "cotters." The family had four children, one deceased. Berhardt and his two younger sisters must have been home-schooled, as the town of Baastad was many miles away. From what we were told, people from the surrounding communities would get together socially a few times a year, and this is where Berhardt met his future wife. As she lived on the opposite side of the lake, he had to row over to court her. Bernhardt was working as a servant in another large home, when the mother and 12-year-old daughter left for America. The husband, Johan, died not long after they left. It was never known if he was sick and told them to go or if he died of a broken heart. Bernhardt followed a couple of years later with his new bride, Anne Marie, their new baby, Carrie, and a sister.

We learned so much that day about the rough times our ancestors had to endure. Ragnhild drove us around to many of the other farms in the area, which lay among beautiful, rolling hills. Most of the fields were planted in mustard, wheat, and other crops. We treated her to lunch after a wonderful day.

Our Norwegian tour wasn't over quite yet. The next day, we left with Sue, Britt, Parrie, and John on a three-day road trip—all planned by Sue. We drove out of town to one of the fjords, and she put us on a ship, while she drove the car to the stop where the ship let us off. We saw villages with their bright-colored houses, waterfalls galore, and lush, green, hillsides. She had a hotel, built in 1700, picked out for us, with more than enough different types of foods. Another night, she had reservations at a rustic pension, way out in the middle of the woods. She drove us to see the Vikings Stave Church, built in 1180. Finally, it was time for us to return return to Oslo. Sue put us onto a fast-moving train in the ski town of Geilo, and we arrived in Oslo at the hotel connected to the Gardemoen Airport. We were on a flight back to Arizona the next morning, after a memorable two-week vacation.

Sitting on "beer rock" in front of our SaddleBrooke home. (I named the rock because, from it, you can see downtown Tucson and the mountains.)

Chapter 29

Living In Arizona

IN 1998, BOTH JILL AND I had retired from the Boeing Company. It was November, and the rain was beginning to bother me. We had rafted the Colorado River in 1993 and were impressed with Arizona, we decided that I would fly down and see if I could find a good location to park our conversion van during the Winter. I arrived in Phoenix and stayed at my cousin's home in Fountain Hills, using it as a base from which to drive around the state. I was returning from Tucson one day when I saw a sign at the base of the Santa Catalina mountains for SaddleBrooke, an active-adult community. Since, I was impressed with the high-desert mountain view, I decided to drive up SaddleBrooke Boulevard and have a look. I located the MountainView swimming pool and asked some residents about life here. They all said it was wonderful! I then went to sales office and talked to the sales people. After looking around some more, I thought that this would be a wonderful place to spend our Winter months. I found a nice lot that I wanted to buy, but the salesman explained that those lots weren't for sale yet. But he gave me a CD about SaddleBrooke, and I brought it back home to show Jill.

A few months later, in February of 2000, Jill and I went to Arizona and stayed for three days. She was very impressed with SaddleBrooke, too. We attended a dinner for prospective residents and later went to the home of the host and hostess and really became enthused about becoming new owners. The next day, we drove around most of the morning and picked out a lot in a newer section, with a southeast view of the mountains. Ours was the sixth home being built in Unit 24. We decided we liked the Loredo-style home, so we drove around for several more days, getting ideas from other homes being built and asking lots of questions. We learned that there were several add-on options. We decided to expand the kitchen by adding a bay window, and we added bay windows in both bedrooms and extended the house an additional three feet. We ordered the back patio to be extended to cover the whole length of the house. And we wanted tile floors throughout the house, except for the bedrooms. We went to the design center to choose various styles of plumbing, electrical outlets, and other add-ons. This was the first new home we had ever had, so it was very exciting. We still had our conversion van, so we did lots of traveling around the area to get familiar with our surroundings. Finally, in November, our home was finished and we drove down for a walk-through. We moved right in, borrowing the mattress from our van, and with little else.

We met the friendly owner of the bakery on Oracle Street, where we went to have sweet rolls the first morning, and he told us we could borrow a plastic table and two chairs until we got our own furniture. We both decided that we wanted to furnish our new home in southwest décor, so we spent many of the next days driving to Tucson to shop for furniture, appliances, lights, etc. We ordered most of our furniture from Lazy Boy, so we had to wait while it was custom made. But we did order a good bed and had it delivered right away. We also bought a small television set for the kitchen. And we had a lot of dishes, pots and pans, and utensils that we had duplicates of from our home up north. Little by little, our new home blossomed into a comfortable domain. It was exciting meeting new neighbors from all over the United States. Every Friday night, we all would go to the MountainView Clubhouse for Happy Hour, and almost every week, we would go to some activity in Tucson or just go exploring around the state. We also participated in several of the SaddleBrooke clubs.

The first one was the bike club, then the hiking club, and later on it would be the swimming club, the computer club, the genealogy club, and the Civil War club. Every month, our unit has a cocktail party at one of the homes, where we all bring beverages and an appetizer. And the group constantly changes, with new people moving in as others move out, so it's always nice to meet our new neighbors. Our completed unit has 143 homes.

We love our Winters in SaddleBrooke. Our home is quite a distance from major traffic, and it's very relaxing in the evenings, sitting out on the back patio. We can hear a pin drop! In SaddleBrooke, the saying is, "When the mountains turn pink, it's time to drink!" Occasionally, a herd of deer or bobcats, javelinas, coyotes, rabbits, road runners or our favorite birds walk through the wash. We enjoy it when the cardinal we nicknamed "Red" would come along with his wife. Early mornings and late evenings, great-horned owls can be heard doing their "hoot hoot" calls. One morning, a wildcat walked right by me while I was drinking my morning coffee. Another time, three baby wildcats were taking naps in our raised flower garden. Pretty soon mama came, and they all jumped down into the wash and hustled on up the hillside. And it always is fun watching the rabbits nibble our carrot peelings.

One of the most exciting aspects of our Laredo-style house is the guest bedroom, facing the Catalina Mountains, which provides us with a multi-purpose viewing area. One evening, Jill and I sat by the bay window watching a quail probe for food beside the extended patio. More soon arrived, marching like soldiers, one behind the other. Next, a Harris Hawk flew down and landed on the patio wall. He was a beautiful specimen. We watched him as he hopped around and then flew off. All the other birds knew he was in the area, and all took shelter upon his arrival! Incidentally, this is the room where I have written most of this book. I spend time there reading and taking a short nap almost every day.

Recently it was our own Happy Hour! We served beer and wine and a German-style dinner of sausages and sauerkraut. As we dined, a low-pressure weather front was moving over the high desert. Silvery, white clouds above the mountain, dropped intermittent rain near the 10,000-foot level, and the sun was setting in the western sky. It projected beams of light on different ridges. Suddenly, a great rainbow formed above the mountains. The clouds changed from gray to purple to pink, and twilight dimmed the sky. We enjoyed our dinner and talked about how lucky we were to live here.

Looking out from our bedroom/den during our daily Happy Hour.

During warmer weather, Jill and I sit outside on the patio for our Happy Hour and to eat breakfast, lunch, and dinner. Most evenings after dinner, we move to the den to watch the news, or movies, or to read. An armoire in the corner holds our computer and printer. Two wooden file cabinets hold most of Jill's genealogy paperwork. We use the living room from time to time to entertain. However, I still think the kitchen has a more relaxed atmosphere.

Swimming as a competitive sport began after we retired and began wintering in Tucson. The SaddleBrooke Swim Club was formed in 2004. My first competition was the Sierra Vista Senior Olympics swimming meet. I was recovering from a cold and was extremely nervous. The first event was a 50-yard freestyle swim. Seven seniors mounted the diving blocks. I thought, "Those are such old fellows that I surely can beat them!" We all dove into the pool, and all I could see were bubbles and waves ahead of me. I finished next to last! My next event was a 200-yard freestyle. I hit the water and swam six laps, but I got tired and was struggling to finish, when the coach yelled, "Keep going, keep going, you have two more laps to go!"

At the Senior Nationals in May of 2019.

Later that year in Tucson, I won the 50-yard freestyle. Our swimming practices are three times a week and I've greatly improved my fitness and skills. In subsequent years, I learned that there were hundreds of things you can do to improve your mind and muscles to become really good. After four years, I was on the 200-yard freestyle relay teams that broke the Arizona State senior Olympics record. As the years passed on, Jill and I won hundreds of swimming medals and subsequently became United States Masters, All-Americans, National Champions, and national record holders. In May of 2019, we swam in the USMS National Swim Meet in Mesa, AZ, where my mixed-relay tean set national records in the 200 freestyle and the 200 medley. And in October, my relay team received two more national records. I was in 10 Top Ten swimming events and won five national championships for the year. Swimming has given both of us great pleasure and has kept us in good physical condition. We're always eager to learn from our great coaches. And we enjoy traveling all over the United States with our swim team and seeing friends and acquaintances at the meets and afterward. We have attended meets in California, Kentucky, Michigan, and Texas over the past 15 years.

In our early days of competition, about 15 years ago.

We also have enjoyed mountain biking since we moved to Arizona. We have favorite trails that we like to ride. One is the "50-Year Trail," originally a cattle trails, which wind through the foothills of the Catalina Mountains, a short drive from our house. Over the years, we've taken a few spills, but in our later years we've been very careful when the trails get rough. One of our other favorite rides is "Willow Springs," where every year on Valentine's Day they have a 24-hour race, where the younger, true mountain bikers ride the 20-mile loop individually or as a team. A third favorite is the "BeeHive," which is also fairly close to home. We keep our old Ford Windstar in the garage, with the bikes mounted on the back, so we can be ready to go at a moment's notice.

T-shirt showing me as Long Distance Champion.

Mountain biking on the 50-year trail, trying to avoid the cacti and rocks!

Our National record-setting relay team, from left,
Coach Doug Springer, Ken McKenny, Al Worth, and me.

Chapter 30

Health

For an octogenarian, I'm pretty healthy, but I'm very strict about getting to the doctor right away if something doesn't feel right. I believe we have to manage our own health. The earliest malady that I recall is earaches—probably caused by colds and congestion. When I was six years old, I had a coughing problem and was taken to the South Haven Hospital, where my tonsils and adenoids were removed, which improved my breathing and cured my coughing. When I was 14, I developed pneumonia and spent a week in the hospital, receiving penicillin shots every three hours. I remember a pretty, blonde nurse who worked third shift. I hardly felt those needles, while I immersed in her good looks and comforting smiles!

During sixth grade, we were introduced to music appreciation. We all were given a plastic, flute-like "tonette," on which we learned to play "All around the cobblers house, the monkey chased the weasel." I didn't pass the hearing test and was not accepted for the middle-school band. Jumping to the age of 36, I drove to the shooting range near Snohomish, WA, to sight-in my hunting rifle. I had just parked my car in the parking lot when an booming, vibrating rifle shot erupted. It hurt my ears, and they began ringing. I went to an ear specialist and he said I had tinnitus (ringing of the ears), for which there is no cure. My ears have been ringing ever since. Since we had no ear protection, the factory noise and aircraft-engine tests at Boeing exacerbated the condition. Now, into my 80s, I have a high-frequency deficiency.

During high school football practice, I broke my little finger. I continued practice, went home, and double-taped the fingers until it healed, which it never really did, as I still have a crooked finger as a reminder. Another time, I probably got a cracked rib playing football but didn't see a doctor. In those days, we just toughed it out! In tackling practice one day, I was hit by Allen Walker and woke up 30 minutes later in the locker room. He was an All-American at the University of Michigan in 1957. Because of my concussion, I didn't play that week and was sent to Kalamazoo for tests. In basketball season, I was in a game at Grand Rapids and was intentionally struck under the chin and saw a snowflake-like mass and asked the coach to take me out of the game. I later returned to play the rest of the game. I'm sure I had another concussion that night. And as I said in the Athletic Chapter, I got a concussion during football practice at Western Michigan University and stayed in the hospital for a week, which ended my football-playing days.

When I was about 50, I was returning from lunch to my job at the Crane Corporation, I was seeing unusual, square-like blocks. Just as I arrived at the door, I became dizzy and weak and collapsed in the doorway. An aide car arrived, and they placed cold towels on my neck. I'd had a minor TIA (Transient Eschimic Attack) stroke. Eleven years later at Boeing, I had another one that resulted in a three-month medical leave of absence. The doctors said these TIAs probably were caused by stress but could have been the result of an irregular-heartbeat condition. Two years later it happened a third time, and shortly afterward I retired from the Boeing Company.

At the beginning of my sophomore year in college, I began wearing glasses for near sightedness. When I was 27 and living in Washington, I was fitted for contact lenses, and 50 years later I underwent Lasik surgery. The result was phenomenal! Never before had I ever been able to see with such the detail and clarity. Six years later, I had cataract surgery that corrected some blurriness. Two years after that, during my annual eye exam, my doctor was suspicious of a possible problem and sent me to another specialist. I had another surgery in my right eye to prevent a detached retina. All of the floaters were removed during that procedure, and my eyesight has improved to where now I have 20/20 vision.

After our son, Kurt, was born I had a vasectomy. During the procedure, unbeknown to me, our family doctor, Dr. Peck, had a son fighting in Viet Nam. My views differed from the doctor's views as we discussed the war—just before he made the cut. Fortunately, I survived with both testicles! Not long after, I was screened by Dr. Forester for carpal-tunnel syndrome in my left wrist. Prior to surgery, I was required to take a prick test. On the day of the procedure at the pre-op discussion, I stopped by the testing office to obtain a copy of the results, after which I gave it to the doctor's receptionist to place into my folder. I then asked the doctor what the test results were. He thumbed through the folder and my test results were not there, but he proceeded with the operation anyway, From that time on, I've always checked to see that nothing was missing or that the proper preparation had been done.

When I was in my early 60s, Dr. Landerholm in Edmonds performed a hernia operation. And when I was 67, he performed a hiatal hernia operation that prevented my stomach contents from entering my esophagus. In my early 70s, Dr. Sheftel took a biopsy of a mole on the back of my neck and found it to be noncancerous. But Dr. Landerholm rechecked it and the biopsy resulted in a diagnosis of Squamous cancer. He removed the mole and found it was benign after all. Since we swim outside in the Winter, Jill and I go to our skin doctor, Dr. Hu, twice a year for checkups. She's removed Squamous cancer from my left ear and right ankle and basal-cell carcinomas from my left hand and thigh. And I've had lots of sprays for pre-cancerous growths on the top of my head and on my ears and arms. She's a top surgeon.

In my mid-70s, I had a colonoscopy and endoscopy (upper digestive tract) on the same day, and I was heavily sedated. The next morning, while Jill was at swim practice, Dr. Tamura called to see how I was doing. I said "OK," and then, all of a sudden, I couldn't talk. Dr. Tamura said, "You're having a heart attack. What's your address?" I couldn't respond, so he immediately called the SaddleBrooke Fire Department, and an aide car was at our house within three minutes. The EMTs applied blood thinners and took me to the emergency room. It took three hours to get my blood pressure restored. We since have learned that colonoscopy and endoscopy procedures should never been performed the same day on older people, due to the effects of too much sedation.

Also in my mid-70s, I began feeling an irregular heartbeat. During swim practice one morning, I over-exerted myself and immediately got out of the pool and into the hot tub. I felt weak and dizzy, so I got out and sat on a bench—but fell onto the cement deck. Jill drove me to the hospital, where it took two hours to bring my heart rate back to near normal. I was diagnosed with A-fib. My primary-care doctor referred me to a heart specialist, who prescribed drugs that didn't agree with me. Later, back in Washington, after changing heart doctors three times, I underwent a cardiac ablation procedure at Swedish Hospital in Seattle that boosted my normal heart rate from 48 to 60 beats per minute. All I do now is take a baby aspirin at bedtime.

In early 2018, after a year of gradually increasing constipation, I was referred to a gastroenterologist. He diagnosed my condition as Anismus, a paradoxical pelvic-floor contraction that comes with age. I do a kind of pelvic exercise that has proved to be very beneficial. Things are now under control, with help from two different types of laxatives I take every morning. But it hasn't slowed down my swimming, and I'm still competing!

In the Spring of 2020, a terrible flu called "coronavirus" spread around the world, causing many deaths. It is very contagious, so it has shut down a lot of businesses, restaurants, sporting events, and parks. And all of the SaddleBrooke pools and other facilities where groups gather were shut down. Jill and I both had flu shots the previous November but still came down with symptoms of the coronavirus flu.

We had sore throats the first day, fevers the next two days, coughs, and wheezing all the way into the lungs. Our noses ran profusely and we used box after box of Kleenex. We stayed mostly indoors, not wanting to pass on whatever we had to neighbors and friends. Jill went to the walk-in clinic and had a lung X-ray, which came back normal.

At the same time, the economy began to shut down, people stayed home, doctor appointments were postponed, face masks were recommended, and other directives were given, especially, "Stay at home!" The virus hit especially hard in Arizona. After six weeks of being sick and finally feeling better, we decided to drive back to Washington. Luckily for us, we were able to spend three nights at our old standby motels along the way, after packing all our meals for the trip and eating them in our room. On the drive, we always washed our hands thoroughly at rest stops. We were happy to arrive at our Priest Point home, where we self-quarantined for two weeks. Luckily, we had plenty of food in our freezer, and Kristie had left the staples in our refrigerator before we arrived. And we had plenty of yardwork to keep us busy for several weeks. We really missed swimming, and after three and one half months of no swimming, we finally were able to swim at a nearby Olympic-size pool, which we've been doing twice a week. We're taking precautions with our face masks, keeping a distance from others, opening windows, and other things. Fortunately, our strong physical conditions have helped to dispel the flu and the coronavirus. At the time of this writing, there is no vaccine for the virus, which became a horrible epidemic.

My dad (1910-1967) and mom (1915-2007).

Chapter 31

Family Connections

I AM REALLY THANKFUL TO MY MOTHER AND FATHER for everything they did for me. Although I was born during the peak of the Great Depression, I never was hungry, I had adequate clothing, I had a bed to sleep in, and I received loving care. While growing up, I took all of these things for granted. Later, when my parents were visiting us in Washington, my dad and I were having a beer together. We were in a good mood and talked about the fun and enjoyment that we had experienced in our lives. During the conversation, I said "Dad, thank you for all you've done for me!" He laughed and handed me six $100 bills and thanked me for a loan I had given him years ago to make the mortgage payment. I said, "You don't have to do that! When I used the family cars, I never had to put gas in them and you helped pay for my college tuition." My dad and mom always had "money management" problems, and he was just beginning to turn their problems around. He was working in Grand Rapids for a plumbing company and making good money and being responsible. He said he always was proud of my sister and me for completing college and having a good, stable life. I'm so glad we had that talk, as I lost my dad in a gas explosion in South Haven in 1967—just two years later.

My stepfather, Sam Tragna, was four years older than my mother. During the early 1930s, he had dated my mother. Unfortunately for him, my father won her love and I became their son. Forty some years later, following my father's death, Sam once again began courting my mother. My mother had other men who were trying to have a permanent relationship, but my brother, sister, and I all preferred Sam. We all knew him from his local grocery store, where he was the butcher and his two brothers ran the other parts of the store. They became engaged and married in 1976. Sam always was a happy Italian guy who would tell good-humored jokes about life. The best one that I remember was, "I dated your mother in 1931, when she was 99 pounds, and I got a bonus of 40 additional pounds to hug in 1976!" Sam and my mother came to Washington twice to visit us. They were married for 15 years, until his death in 1990. I flew back to South Haven when he was diagnosed with cancer. My parting words were, "I love you, Pop."

My mother and stepfather, Sam Tragna.

I was fortunate to have a wonderful sister, Adelaide, who was born eight years after me. And eight years after her, my brother, Tom, was born. Adelaide and her late husband, Dick, had retired to Marco Island in Florida, so we don't see each other nearly enough. Adelaide always has been very talented and artistic. She is quite the sculptor. She carved three gila monsters out of a large, African rock that we have proudly displayed in our Arizona home. She had shipped it to us in 2014, after taking two years to complete. Tom also was a plumber, like his father and grandfather, and also is retired and lives in South Haven with his wife, Cathy, and two sons.

"Tom, Dick, and Harry"—
my brother, Tom, my brother-in-law, Dick, and my father, Harry.

My paternal grandmother and grandfather Fritz always were very supportive, providing my family homemade bread, borrowed cars, and part-time work during the Depression. In earlier years, it was quite a challenge raising six boys. They all turned out well, four plumbers, a vice president of Citizens Bank, and the owner of an insurance company. I liked all of my uncles and their wives and especially my cousins.

I also enjoyed my grandparents on my mother's side, Claude and Edith Rogers. During the Depression, we would visit them in Glen, just outside South Haven. In 1944, my grandfather, a carpenter, helped renovate our house on Park Avenue. In 1967, they loaned my parents $9,000 to buy a Cape Cod-style home on the shore of Lake Michigan.

The Richard Pence family—Nancy, Dick, my sister, Adelaide, and Robert.

Jill's parents were like my second set of parents, in that they were part of my life for 45 years, compared with the 25 years I lived in South Haven. Jill and I were fortunate to have enjoyed the fun times at their house, where the kids could swim and the families would get together. They loaned us $5,000 when we were between jobs, which provided us with house payments for almost one year. And I definitely want to mention Jill's uncle Frank. He helped us fix washing machines and dryers in the apartment building over the years, when they needed repair. He and his wife, Olive, were happy people. He was very generous and loaned money to Jill's father to help him finish building the Johnson Apartments.

Now, saving the best for last, I want to talk about our own two children, Kristie and Kurt. Kristie always is so positive and loving and helpful to everyone, especially us. She always was involved in high school sports and club activities, which developed her qualities of organization and responsibility. She acquired a strong work ethic while still in high school, working in fast-foods restaurants and at Anthony's on the Everett waterfront. After high school, she enrolled at Edmonds Community College and received a two-year Travel/Tourism degree. She continued working at restaurants and sports bars, making more money on tips than on wages. She then obtained her two-year Associated Arts degree from Seattle Community College and transferred to the University of Washington, where she majored in Liberal Arts, with an emphasis on Environmental studies. She received her four-year degree in 1992.

Our daughter, Kristie, ready for work, with her beloved VW bug and Gulfstream jet.

While going to college, Kristie was one of the first female waitresses in the main dining room during lunch at the Columbia Tower Club, a private dining club in downtown Seattle. She also worked as a teller at Seafirst Bank for four years during and after college. After college, she took a few solo trips through Europe, having picked up the travel bug from us! She then worked on four different private yachts as a stewardess for two years, which took her all through the Panama Canal, the Caribbean, the Mediterranean, and several crossings of the

Atlantic Ocean. She then became a flight attendant for four years on a corporate Gulfstream for a private family based in Seattle. She now has been flying for 19 years for Netjets, where she works one week on and one week off. She has owned her own home for 20 years in Edmonds and has a beautiful English garden, which is her passion on her week off. She loves to entertain, especially around her bonfire. And when it's cooler outside, she has blankets and warm coats for everyone. She has many great friends and neighbors, who she's always reaching out to and helping. She clearly enjoys her life in Edmonds very much.

Our son, Kurt.

Our son, Kurt, was especially ambitious when he turned 16. He worked nights at Safeway, stocking food shelves and retrieving carts from the parking lot. He saved enough money to buy his first car. After high school, he worked aboard a purse seiner in southeast Alaska during the Summer and for a cement contractor during the Winter. After several years, he joined the Davis-Schuller Construction

Company and has worked his way up to construction manager, which regularly requires him being on the job more than 48 hours a week. We don't know how he did it, given his work demands and raising two children, but he built a beautiful family home in the country.

Kurt and his wife, Sherri, divorced after 25 years of marriage and their children were out on their own. Both are good people, but unfortunately their goals and personalities were not a perfect match. A couple of years after Kurt's divorce, his friends had a surprise 50th birthday party for him, and, Wendy, one of his old schoolmates, who also was recently divorced, attended. They have been enjoying each other's company ever since. Soon they were taking Kurt's boat to Hat Island, where Wendy owns a small cabin on the beach. The project to fix up the cabin provided them with energy and positive achievements. It's nice to see Kurt's happiness. Wendy is now part of our family, and we love them both dearly.

I want to tell Kristie and Kurt how much I love and admire them for what they've done with their successful lives and thank them for helping us and other people.

Our grandchildren, Kortney and Hunter.

Kurt and Sherri's daughter, Kortney, was our first grandchild, born in Providence Hospital in Everett. She was a cute baby. In junior high school, she belonged to 4-H and raised several pigs. Then she played basketball and volleyball at Lakewood High School, near their home. She was an honor-roll student and gained a whole year of college credits when she was a senior. She went on to Washington State University, graduating with a bachelor's degree in Science. I admire her work ethic, since she also had an evening job at a pizza restaurant all through college. She still lives in Pullman and is employed by a company that manufactures high-capacity electrical-generating systems. We're proud of her hard work and accomplishments.

Hunter is our other grandchild, born in Everett, also. He has worked as a commercial fisherman and attended Everett Junior College for two years. He's now a maritime apprentice, working on the Everett waterfront. From our home on Priest Point, we can watch his tugboats go out to meet freighters or military ships and escort them in. Hunter is very positive, and we love him to death! He always says, "Everything is good!" He's quite the hunter, be it birds, deer, elk, bear, whatever. And he loves fishing. He lives close by and can launch his boat into Puget Sound in Marysville.

Hunter is in the process of choosing a career field. This is good, because I know I changed majors three times in college and three times afterward. I'm trying to help him in finding an appropriate career field. I will suggest that he join the local Junior Chamber of Commerce. When I lived on Mercer Island in my bachelor days, I joined, and it provided me an opportunity for service to the community and to achieve objectives. The Snohomish Public Utility District should welcome this background, since Hunter is hoping to get a foot in the door there. He has a very out-going personality, is caring about others and is not afraid of taking on new challenges. Whatever he chooses as a career, I'm sure we will be successful. However, he may have to curtail some of his hunting and fishing activities when he finds the right job!

From left, brother Tom, mom, sister Adelaide, and me at mom's 80th birthday celebration in South Haven.

The sculpture that my sister, Adelaide, carved for us.

Daughter, Kristie.

Grandson, Hunter, me, son, Kurt, and Pauline Lindahl, our best friend and neighbor for 50 years.

Brother, Tom Fritz, and family—
Shawn, my mother, Venita, Tom's wife, Cathy, Nate, Tom, and Matt.

Chapter 32

The Future

I CAN'T FORESEE EXACTLY WHAT THE FUTURE will bring, but here are some of the critical aspects—as I see them now. There are too many world conflicts that could lead to wars. We have global warming. We have ocean pollution. We have job losses from robotics and artificial intelligence. Amazon is killing small businesses. Our infrastructure is old, overstressed, and deteriorating. Healthcare and drug costs are escalating. People on illegal and addictive drugs are destroying our country. The increasing incarceration of people is costing billions of dollars. Our federal government's purposes and processes need to be addressed. Productivity needs to be defined and taught to everyone. Legislation should not have add-ons that are not related to the main bill. And lobbying should be banned.

But more important than all of the above, is world over-population. Excessive population increases have caused pollution, global warming, and increased crime and debt around the globe. Zero population growth should be a target for the future. Fifty years ago, the *Readers Digest* ran an article written by a university economics professor. Before I describe what he said, I want to interject something I learned about conference leadership. The leader first identifies the objectives of the meeting. Secondly, he or she determines who should attend, An excessive number of attendees makes agreement more difficult and extends the timeline for completing the work that needs to be accomplished.

In that regard, the professor stated that our federal government has too many people. Too much time is spent haggling over differences among politicians from 50 states. His suggestion was to reduce the 50 states to six, representing homogeneous regions of the country. He said that by removing excessive people from the discussions, more positive results would occur. And as we're moving from the information to the artificial-intelligence age, let's look way off into the future, say 2050. I foresee time when almost no one will need to work. Robots will plan, organize, and manage our basic needs. Those who are better educated—and that includes doctors and scientists—will be given credits or vouchers for their contribution to the robotic output. The inventor types also will be compensated for their creations.

Epilogue

I've been lucky to have good parents, preachers, teachers, professors, mentors, supervisors, coaches, and consultants to help me throughout my life. I would like to share with you some of the following concepts that they have given me.

Always look to improve yourself. As I stated before, work is the pathway to success. However, "knowledge" provides the tools along the way, and "experience" sharpens the skill sets. You must continually build new bridges of knowledge, through learning from mentors or educational institutions. College is important but not always necessary.

Here are two examples. Jill's high school classmate, Doug Boseck, began working at a Green Lake bicycle-repair shop and followed in the footsteps of the owner. He later became a partner in the largest equipment-rental business in Washington state. And our friend, Carl Larsen, began as a laborer for Snohomish County. After marrying his wife, Sharon, he worked with his father to build their first home, and Carl learned that he could build houses by himself. He began by building small houses and gradually built larger ones, as well as commercial buildings. Meanwhile, Sharon took business courses, and together they became a successful team in their own construction company.

Whatever field you choose, be deeply dedicated to it. If you need to change careers or jobs, look for ones that complement your education and experience. Sometimes you might have to accept temporary employment if you're laid off. But always aspire to move from that low point to the highest possible road for you journey.

There are lots of decisions in life and many paths to choose. The important considerations are whether a choice is "reasonable," "feasible" and "achievable." Always pursue achievement with positive thoughts, like "good," "better" and "best." Filter out "bad," "awful" and "worst." It takes hard work and commitment to make a project successful. "Collaboration"—the sharing of ideas and work—is the best way to move more rapidly toward successful results.

Whether in personal relationships or in business, think "creating and building" rather than "destroying and dismantling." At Boeing, I was creating cost-cutting methods, at Western Gear, I was creating jobs and at Prudhoe Bay, I was creating safe work environments, You also need to be creative when you encounter obstacles, like strained relationships or layoffs. If there's no complete solution, then you must plan how you can "manage the situation."

Don't be afraid to take risks when there is an opportunity to do something challenging. To illustrate, Jill and I did that when we saw the chance to buy her parents' apartment building in 1980. I asked Jill to tell her parents that we were interested in having them sell the apartment to us. Jill was apprehensive and delayed asking them for about two years, only to find out that they thought it was a good idea. Her parents also benefited by having us near to help care for them until they died. As I've said, without the income from the apartment building, we never would have been able to have our Winter home in SaddleBrooke.

The world would be in pretty bad shape if everyone didn't practice a degree of "conformity." If people failed to comply with laws and government, everything would be chaotic. Compliance means following direction and designated policies and procedures. Whether we like it or not, nearly everyone has a supervisor or boss. He or she is responsible to his/her boss and it passes on up the line. Failure to follow directions can get you fired or jailed for an unlawful offense.

Some of the other aids that I acquired from my Training and Development career include the five Ws—who, what, when, where, and why. To become a good listener, you need to remember that, in a conversation, the other person has a thought or story to tell, too. If you interrupt after the "who or what," you've denied the speaker his total input. You also should be conscious of the five W's when expressing something to more than one person. And whenever you want commitment from others, remember the words timing, patience, and diplomacy. Patience is the area where I have had the toughest time. I also learned to appreciate ideas from college interns, who I often hired to assist with company projects.

I learned in a character-education class in college that love is "self-giving"—not expecting anything in return—and that the most important quality is "physical giving"—taking every opportunity to assist your family and community. Make it a habit to ask others, "How may I help you?," rather than, "Why should I help you?" Remember, in life there are hills that go up—and hills that go down. Never lose faith—regroup, plan, and persist in carrying out what you need to do.

I wish all of you a successful life, full of love, work, and play.

Acknowledgments

I ESPECIALLY WOULD LIKE TO THANK my wife, Jill, for the excellent job she did in putting my writings and photos into the computer. We got computer assistance from Monty at Monty's PC Solutions and Richard Spitzer from the SaddleBrooke Computer Club. Both gave us helpful instructions and training on placing and captioning the photos. Our grandson, Hunter, was instrumental in guiding us throughout our final stages. An extra big "thank you" to our good friend and swimming coach, Phil Simpson, for all the proofreading that he did for us and for correcting many spelling and punctuation errors. And I am extremely appreciative of the professionalism and patience shown by Larry Coffman, Melissa Coffman and Scott Book in guiding us through the editing, layout and placement of photos and captions.

www.ingramcontent.com/pod-product-compliance
Lightning Source LLC
Chambersburg PA
CBHW071959110526
44592CB00012B/1141